AM I
CLEVER
OR AM I
STUPID?

AM I CLEVER OR AM I STUPID?

RACHÉ RUTHERFORD
KOBUS NEETHLING

BOOKS

Carpe Diem Books • Vanderbijlpark • South Africa
Inspiration for Mind, Body and Soul

Our mission at Carpe Diem Books:

To proclaim the Word of God with sincerity and with Christ's authority, as commissioned and sent by God (2 Corinthians 2:17), and to equip believers who wish to be practising Christians.

For more information on new books, Prisma Book Club, authors, special offers, Send a Gift Book, daily devotions and finesse magazine, visit our web site: www.carpediem.co.za

© 2001 Carpe Diem Books
PO Box 5801 Vanderbijlpark 1900
Tel • (016) 982–3617
Fax • (016) 982–3618
E-mail • info@carpediem.co.za

Second edition, twelth print 2001
ISBN 1-919818-56-1

Typesetting • Griselda Lottering
Editor • San-Mari Mills
Cover design • Helga la Grange
Printing • Creda Communications

Contents

Icons

Activity

Narrative

Important information

Jenny was 52 years old. She had been an administrative clerk in a bank for 30 years and seemed quite happy with her circumstances. But when she walked into my practice that day she told me about a dream she had harboured for more than 10 years – a book-exchange shop of her own. Yet she had done nothing to pursue and achieve this goal.

She had no academic qualifications, she did not believe she was particularly intelligent and she had not achieved anything really meaningful in her life. So Jenny woke up with her dream every morning, but every morning she was the one to shatter it, telling herself there was no way she could realise this dream.

However, once Jenny's "I can't do it, it's not for me," was transformed into "I can, it is possible," she began to realise that not only one intelligence exists, that there are many more than the academic and intellectual intelligences we traditionally believed to be the essence of success and achievement. When she started discovering her own other intelligences, new ideas and alternatives started taking the place of her normal negative talk.

Today Jenny has a flourishing business of her own. She is an achiever! It took her more than 50 years to realise that she is clever and competent, that she is competitive and able, that it is possible to accomplish her dreams.

There are many Jennies out there who think they are stupid and believe they *cannot*.

We want you to *think* and *do* as you read through this book. It does not matter who you are, how old you are and where you're from, you *can* make your dreams come true. You have the right and the ability to shake hands with a better tomorrow.

– Kobus Neethling and Raché Rutherford –

This book is about redefining the terms 'clever' and 'stupid'. It is about gaining or rediscovering those thinking skills which can set you free from the narrow confines of your present moorings and enable you to embark on an exciting journey of self-discovery, and ultimately, self-fulfilment.

But it has a much deeper dimension. It is a practical, self-help book which, as you work through it, will reveal to you more and more about yourself. It will help you realise that you are unique, that you are clever and creative in your own special way. As you become aware of your own unique strong points, your confidence will grow.

This book, if used correctly, will broaden your mind, improve your self-knowledge and thinking skills, your tolerance towards others who differ from you. It will build your self-confidence and make you realise that it is not too late to become the person who has until now, existed in your dreams only.

Introducing a new kind of Clever and Stupid for a new kind of Human Being

Since the beginning of time every generation has developed its own particular knowledge and skills to manage its immediate world and circumstances. Insight and understanding gained from managing the todays and learning from the past, have formed the cornerstones of education and training through the ages. The future was projected and understood in terms of past and present information. Five and ten year plans, goals and visions were developed and based on what we understood about today and what we had learnt from the past.

The explosive nature of the latter part of the 20th century, forced us to re-examine and reassess most of our definitions about the past, future and present; it forced us to redefine many of our beliefs which were deemed to be sacred, and it forced us to take a good, long look at ourselves – our skills, our behaviour, our creativity and our wisdom.

The diagram below shows how dramatically the 21st century differs from all the previous centuries and that if we do not become different human beings, we will not survive the onslaught of change.

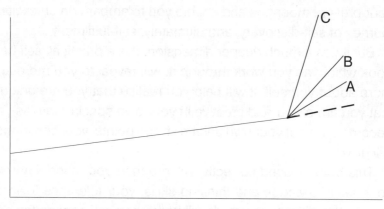

Most of the meaningful predictions since the middle of the twentieth century indicated that the future would start arriving much quicker than ever before. Toffler talked about future shock and he predicted that the tempo of change would not follow the dotted line of our curve, but would shoot up to point A. In the nineteen eighties there was even greater acceleration as the future started to arrive from new and unforeseen directions and at a tempo that exceeded the predictions of most futurists. For a short time point B was the focus of individuals and organisations until the biggest revolution in modern history (and possibly of all time) started to alter every definition regarding business, education, empowerment, media – a list that would fill all the pages of this book. At the arrival of the Internet the original Toffler curve rocketed to a point C and beyond, and words and concepts like the following started to dominate:

- e-business

- e-education
- e-learning
- e-preaching
- e-students
- e-selling
- e-communication

e-dictionaries are already on the market introducing a new vocabulary and a new language. For many individuals, families and organisations the future looks ominous, because so many of the anchors of the past seem to be fragile and wavering.

Changing your Perspective

Because it will become increasingly difficult to predict the exact content of the future; the direction of technology, the "right" products, the "best" qualifications, the "most lucrative" investments and just about everything else, success and happiness will depend less on your accurate predictions of the future and much more on the content and direction of your own psyche.

Two of the words used most frequently to describe (and more often to label) people according to the way they are perceived to be achieving, are "clever" and "stupid". For centuries these two words were defined in very narrow terms and in most instances the way of thinking about these two intimidating descriptions was formed and refined during the formal school years. You were labelled, or you labelled others according to their scholastic achievements – the more A symbols, the more brilliant you were perceived to be; the more E and F symbols, the more stupid you were deemed to be and the more remarks were made about your lack of intelligence.

The sad thing about this kind of labelling is that it does not seem to go away. Ten, twenty, thirty years after you have left school you still fall within the clever, average or stupid category in the eyes of old school friends or teachers – and often also in your own eyes. It does not matter if you are now a successful business person, designer, computer specialist or whatever; it seems that in the thinking of the 20th century human being, clever referred to high school marks, academic excellence in particularly selected subject areas like Mathematics, Natural Sciences and a few others, and very little beyond this narrow definition.

The authors are not for one moment implying that skills in Mathematics and the Natural Sciences or distinctions in general, are less important now than in previous centuries, but what we are emphasising is that we look far beyond the narrow paradigms of the past for talent, intelligence, creativity and for "clever". Parents, teachers, trainers, coaches, managers, and every person involved in the empowerment of others need to develop a special ability to sense where things are going and be tuned to what is really "clever" and what is really "stupid" in the 21st century. The future will keep on rocketing towards us, information will keep on coming from every possible direction and there will be no escape routes for those who cannot adjust to these explosive times.

The 21st century is however not a bad news century; on the contrary, it is the century of hope and opportunity for all people who are open to continuous transformation and the surpassing of our known existence. Yes, the skills which dominated 20th century education, business, leadership and just about everything else will still be important and even vital in particular circumstances *but* beyond

- the logic
- the rational and analytical thinking
- the linear and organised focus
- the clinical and critical approach
- the traditional and experienced
  the other focus will be on
- imagination
- intuition
- looking for alternatives
- risk taking

- the big picture
- image streaming
- meaningful forgetting
- integration and connection
- passion, energy and courage

and eventually the genius and the very clever will be those who are able to use their whole brain to create the possibilities and the solutions that will enable you to take back your dream and restore significant purpose and passion to your life.

"Change must become the norm, not cause for alarm. The bottom line is: if you cannot point to something specific that is being done differently from the way it was done when you came to work this morning, you surely have not earned your pay cheque by any stretch of the imagination."

– Tom Peters –

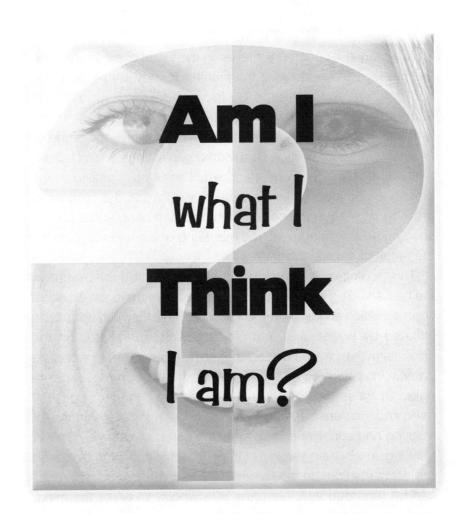

Chapter 1

Before embarking on a journey which increasingly deepened my interest in the world of creativity, I had the privilege to be involved in teaching for several years. I also had golden opportunities to do focused research on the child and the process of growing up. This interest did not wane as I gradually moved into the adult's way of thinking, the world of business, industry, politics, sport and organisations. I don't believe that it is possible to understand adult thinking, behaviour and emotions completely, unless there is insight into the process of growing up. Although specific moments can bring about unique shaping and development, the moulding of a person is normally the result of several processes.

This book certainly does not attempt to explain the psyche of the human being in complicated terminology – there are excellent sources which do just that. *The Psychology of the mind* approach, initiated by Roger Mills and George Pransky, focuses on the conclusion that psychological functioning rests on three principles, namely the mind, a person's thinking and his or her consciousness. Of these three, only thinking can be changed; both the mind and the consciousness are fixed. The mind is the source of thinking and consciousness, while the consciousness embodies thinking; in a certain sense it clarifies your thoughts. An overhead projector, the light on the screen and the overhead transparency can be regarded as three parts of a whole. Likewise the mind, thoughts and consciousness can be regarded as one. The overhead projector is fixed (the mind causing the light to shine); the light on the screen is fixed (consciousness making thoughts visible to the outside world); and then the only part that can change is the overhead transparency (thinking). Each time a new transparency appears on the screen and the light of the overhead projector shines on it, a new message is projected.

Because you can change your thinking, you can change virtually everything. No reality exists until your thoughts make it real. Two people standing next to each other can look at the same apple – one might see it as a delicious fruit while the other can't stand the taste of it. It remains the same fruit, but it is nothing until your thoughts change it into something. Therefore the essence of the human being's existence is not the circumstances a person finds him or herself in, but the way this person *thinks about* these circumstances. This explains why some people remain cool, calm and collected in the worst crises, while others become excited and hysterical in the same situations. Because you are the thinker of your own thoughts it is always possible to keep those thoughts positive and cheerful. The way in which you judge and evaluate yourself governs the image you project to the outside world. If you are continually negative and derogatory about yourself and regard yourself as inferior, you are hampering your particular and versatile possibilities. If you think you cannot achieve this or that, this closed, restrained thinking eventually restrains behaviour and achievement. You think yourself stupid and you allow circumstances (including other people) to convince you that you are.

Stupid and clever are words that must be seen in context. This is a fundamental truth, a fact which each parent, teacher and mentor must acknowledge and understand as the first step in human development. Leaders, managers and supervisors daily find themselves in circumstances where clever and stupid are enacted all the time – within a certain context. Stupid and clever manifest themselves in a variety of forms and guises:

• the inability to do what you yourself have identified as something that needs to be done; that which someone else requested or ordered; or knowing that you are able to do what you are being confronted with (category 1);
• uncertainty about the task you have to perform, or the certainty that you will be able to perform it successfully (category 2);

- moments of helplessness and impotence, or moments of exceptional clarity and insight (category 3);
- a general (more or less embracing) feeling that you fail at most of (or all) the things you do, or an overall certainty that you can accomplish almost anything successfully (category 4).

These categories can be divided into further sub-categories, but for our purpose and focus the above-mentioned classification is sufficient. The process preceding each of the above-mentioned manifestations differs in detail, intensity, scope and nature from one individual to another, but there are definitely common factors characterising each one in particular, and others which contain characteristics of all the categories. Let us take a moment to consider the various categories and find out why you sometimes find yourself in one or more of them.

 The knowledge (ability) or lack of knowledge (inability) to perform a specific task

Where does this **ability** come from? It usually comes from an inherent conviction that you possess the expertise and/or the insight to carry out a specific assignment. This stems from a background of training and/or experience, a proven record of success or potential success, or an intuitive feeling that you can accomplish the task. One, or a combination of these factors can contribute towards creating, developing, or maturing this ability.

Where does the **inability** come from? In most cases inability is the result of a process that can start at any time, and can develop either slowly or dramatically. It can start at school where the child's scholastic performance does not come up to expectations as a result of a variety of factors. Reasons for such failure to perform are usually intellectual inability (a low IQ and low marks in specific school subjects), laziness, circumstances at home, and resistance to learning. Once again it can be due to either one, or a combination of factors. However, when you look at the essence of each of these factors, there are often hidden processes in operation which are ignored or just go unnoticed. I would like to highlight a few of these behind-the-scenes processes:

• A battery of intelligence tests are essential for accurate results. The single conventional test can thus produce results that are insufficient to ascertain intellectual ability in its wider scope and meaning. This occurs especially in a contemporary world that makes radically different demands with regard to the intellect, and which is in fact looking for a new kind of intelligence. Paul Torrance has indicated that if we continue with our conventional and often useless measuring procedures, we exclude about 72% of our creative potential, because provision is not made for creativity and innovative thinking in the standard measuring procedures.

• Laziness and resistance to learning can certainly be just that, but the reasons for these phenomena can be a complex intertwining of factors. I acknowledge the resistance-disposition that characterises the growing up process, but this acceptance does not mean that laziness and resistance to learning must be accepted as an inevitable part of the learning process. The stimulation, the passion which accompanies tuition, the dynamics of the environment in which tuition and learning take place, as well as other factors that apparently have little to do with the learning content, are fundamental to the understanding and interpretation of laziness.

• The reaction of the mentor (who can be the parent, teacher and later on the manager or supervisor) can feed the feeling of inability to such an extent that the person, child or adult, will later experience inability (stupidity) as a premise.

Certainty or uncertainty about

performing a specific task

Certainty about your ability to perform a specific task comes from experience or expertise in that field, and the level of certainty depends on a proven record of success within that particular field. The certainty can also come from success achieved in related fields, in which case skills and expertise can then be transferred. For example, if you have been very successful in the manufacturing of beds, you will perform the task of making beds with confidence. It is also possible that you will be equally confident when given the task to make chairs, as you will realise that the skills required to make beds and chairs are very similar. The more this suppleness is developed in the thinking process, the better people will understand that **certainty** is possible in many more areas than generally believed.

Uncertainty about the ability to execute a specific task is usually found when particular expertise or experience is lacking. This kind of uncertainty can be the result of one factor, or a combination of factors:

● It is a new field and falls outside the familiar environment – hence the uncertainty whether the known skills and insights can be transferred to the new field.

● The task falls within the scope of the bigger framework of the work description, but the nature, intensity or degree of difficulty differs. For example, as a real estate agent you have sold an average of three houses per month in a specific area; now you are expected to sell six houses per month – a difference in intensity. Or you are asked to sell factories when in the past you have only sold residential property – now the nature of the task changes. You can be asked to make projections as to what kind of property will be sold in future and where and when – the degree of difficulty is possibly increased by such a request. Hence you are not *continually* uncertain, but you are uncertain in *specific situations*. The more you are confronted with this kind of situation, the more *specific* uncertainties become *constant* uncertainty if you do not realise what essential thinking processes are required here. And the result? Once again a feeling of stupidity.

Moments of clarity versus moments of helplessness

This category differs from the previous one in the sense that moments of insight or of powerlessness cannot necessarily be explained. It can be in a person's nature to often have a sort of 'aha'-experience, which is then accepted as a matter of course. Conversely, a moment, or moments of 'aha' can be experienced by someone whom nobody expects it from (because this person has not demonstrated it before, or because conventionally, 'aha'-experiences are not expected from certain people or they are thought incapable of this.) There can be more than one explanation of these moments, the most common one being that intuitive wisdom brings clarity. Intuitive wisdom is when knowledge, experience, insight and creativity combine in the mind in a unique manner, and this combination then creates 'aha'-experiences. Intuition is also a skill which can be developed by all of us.

In the same way, moments of helplessness can be experienced by people who are normally sharp and clear in their reactions, but who experience insight-blockages in certain situations. It sometimes happens for example, that students who usually do well in mathematics, experience moments of helplessness when writing an examination, and consequently perform far below their usual standard. This helplessness often occurs in very specific situations:

- in certain environments (classroom, office of the manager, etc.);
- in the presence of certain people (school principal, supervisor, one of your heroes, etc.);
- unexpected confrontations (a sudden change of plan, routine changes, for example something which is not in its usual place, a road map which does not indicate all the streets, etc.).

Helplessness of this kind must always be placed in perspective. Although these moments of helplessness differ in nature and scope from person to person, they are experienced by all people. It has to do with the context of the moment and the way the mind handles that context, not what is traditionally classified as 'stupid' and 'clever' categories.

The overall feeling of knowing that you do almost everything well, or contrary to this, the feeling that you do nothing well

This conviction that you can accomplish almost everything successfully can also be a delusion – a sort of false evaluation of yourself which only you believe, and no one else. This is not what I am talking about. I am referring to an overall feeling of knowing that you can do almost anything successfully and that you have good reason to think so – preferably within an acceptable attitude-context. (I realise that 'acceptable' also has more than one connotation.) This sort of knowledge can be created when the child performs well at an early stage (not necessarily with regard to the extraordinary, but especially with regard to everyday things), and is consequently encouraged and supported all the time.

Learning security manifests itself, and further dimensions develop from this, when risks are built into the child's world. These risks are initially managed by a mentor until the child can handle them in the same way he handles the familiar: with confidence. This sort of knowledge can develop later, when the person's experience of his world has widened to such an extent that he is able to handle the new variety of situations in his life with the same ease that he dealt with the less complicated ones. When one continuously experiences and handles different circumstances in a planned manner, unexpected situations are not alarming when they suddenly crop up – the knowledge that also the unexpected can be handled successfully has already been established. Fact remains however, that humans are unique beings, and because of this, we have to make choices about the circumstances we prefer in the end. It is possible to handle almost all circumstances successfully, but not all of them will arouse the same passion. There are certain things you like more than others and this will and should determine your choices or preferences.

It is also important to emphasise here that no person can be an expert in every field. Knowing that you can do anything successfully acknowledges this premise and therefore you know this as well. For example, if I am asked to build a house, I know that I can complete the project successfully, although I have very little knowledge of roofing and brickwork. I realise that, in order to accomplish the task successfully, certain expertise has to be brought in.

In the same way that the general feeling develops that you can be successful at anything, the negative conviction that you cannot do anything properly also develops. The following are the most common reasons for this feeling:

- no encouragement from parents, mentors and other people involved in the growing-up process;
- continual focus on the negative and destructive;
- labelling as a result of minor errors (small mistakes which are blown up out of proportion, and used out of context);
- no support in moments of hesitance and uncertainty;
- very little understanding from educators as to what is essential

to the learning process and what is not;
- not enough differentiation in learning styles and receptiveness of children (despite the difference in receptivity, everybody is taught in the same manner);
- despondency as a result of a process which is becoming more intense (if meaningful intervention does not put a stop to this);
- handling staff too autocratically, and breaking down individual initiative can lead to a feeling of helplessness and inferiority.

This list can certainly be supplemented, but here we find the basic elements of the process leading to a lack of confidence, a feeling of complete helplessness and loss of self-respect.

Establishing 'clever' and 'stupid'

All the processes discussed above, can lead to the conviction that:

- I am stupid, I must accept it and live accordingly;
- I am stupid most of the time;
- I am a little stupid;
- I experience moments of stupidity.

The tragic consequences of this *stupid-classification* are that you gradually convince yourself that you cannot accomplish what you would like to. Your ideals become impossibilities, you start accepting second and third best and regard happiness and achievement as worlds beyond your reach, something only meant for other people. Because you have come to this conclusion **in your mind**, it follows that it can also be reversed **in your mind**. The wonderful thing about this is that each and every one of us can change our thoughts and our way of thinking, and eventually also our emotions and behaviour, so that in the end we find new meaning in life and are able to achieve that which has always been out of reach.

This process can certainly result in different levels of 'feeling clever', and make this a reality in your life.

It is true that the influence of the mentor, the parent, the teacher and the environment can be more formative, intense and pre-dominant during the pre-school stage and through adolescence than when it is manifested in the adult world. But when adults still experience this feeling of being stupid, they have allowed their circumstances to dominate them, instead of allowing their minds to exercise positive control over their circumstances. Of course it is also true of a child, but the influence of circumstantial factors must be placed within an adult-child perspective. If my circum-stances at home are miserable, if my parents give me no support, my school environment is depressing and I have no positive con-nections with family or friends, then the 'stupid' connotation in all its confusing forms can have a major impact on my thinking.

The adult ought to (I repeat, **ought to**) make a clearer differen-tiation between the *circumstances*, the external factor, and the *thinking* that should govern that external factor. This factor can be a person: a partner, a member of the family, a manager who is always negative in his/her criticism. The external factor can also be a discouraging or depressing environment which supports conformity and the mundane, and steadily breaks down the soul of the human being. If your reaction to external factors makes you feel inferior, good for nothing, then your thinking has indeed started dropping below the line. You have allowed your thinking to become restricted, to be overpowered, and eventually you have begun to accept the image of a dunce. Only you can bring about a reversal, by deciding to start thinking above the line, by changing your negativity into a positive approach, and by realising that you were not born negative, gloomy or stressed-out. These are unnat-ural conditions which you have created in your own mind – and you will also have to make the transformation within your own mind.

Once you start realising that your thoughts come from your own mind, that you have created them yourself, you can also start to address your (own!) conditioned thinking. Conditioned

thinking can occur with regard to any possible person or thing:
- You do not like a certain person, because you have experienced, seen or heard something about that person. As a result you have formed certain ideas about him or her. (One of your colleagues may feel completely different about the same person because he or she experiences ths person differently.)
- At some stage in your life you had an experience with a certain kind of food and as a result you have negative thoughts about this food and consequently refuse to eat it.
- At a specific moment in your life, you formed certain thoughts about particular politicians, resulting in 'pro' or 'anti' thoughts.
- At school you had an unpleasant experience with a certain teacher or subject, which gave rise to feelings of inability.

In all these cases – and each one of us can certainly draw up similar lists – conditioning has stifled creative and flexible thinking. Preconceived thoughts, which were probably real and genuine while living through a specific experience, have deprived us of the opportunity to think about this experience in a new and dynamic way. We believe and know, and don't attempt fresh thoughts about a certain issue. The repetition of destructive thinking patterns makes them habit. (It started with a thinking process and can also be eliminated by one!) A malfunction in the thinking process can cause some people to worry about trivialities and eventually they are never without worries of some kind. Their way of thinking does not choose joy, but misery – habitual misery.

In the same way you can start thinking and believing that you are stupid. You are conditioned to function in an awkward, helpless and stupid manner by the way you think about certain experiences in your life. You no longer react with new thoughts, but with your habitual way of thinking which makes you believe you can't. And this insecurity often leads to even greater insecurities which force you to fall back on old thinking frames of reference.

The process of rediscovery

In the following chapters you are not only sent on a creative journey of discovery, but at the same time you are asked to rediscover yourself. Keep an open mind throughout; don't allow preconceived thoughts to prevent you from looking at knowledge and skills with a fresh pair of eyes. You will rediscover the **clever** in yourself which you have already on occasion, or repeatedly, utilised and experienced. But even more important: you will discover other forms, facets and uniqueness of **clever**, which you were not even aware of and which have probably remained hidden by a variety of factors.

The following case studies focus on the variety of the rediscovery process and on how different people have been renewed and changed in different ways; how they have freed themselves from the shackles of restriction and inferiority – ordinary people who have started to realise that you are your own worst restricting factor and that you, who have built the walls, can also break them down.

Narrative

Priscilla Ward

Priscilla left school in the eleventh grade. She had never done well at school and in the second half of her Grade 11 year her schoolwork deteriorated even more. She failed two subjects and after a discussion with her parents they decided to take up the matter with the teachers. It was decided that Priscilla would leave school. Priscilla regarded herself as stupid because of her poor scholastic performance since starting high school. Without directly supporting this viewpoint, her teachers did little or nothing to change this perception she had of

herself. Priscilla saw her E and F symbols as proof of her stupidity and so did her teachers. Within the context of the school environment this evaluation could possibly have been correct (but keep in mind the four categories discussed earlier in this chapter under the heading *Establishing 'clever' and 'stupid'* in order to understand also this context correctly).

After leaving school Priscilla started working as an administrative clerk for an insurance company. Three years later she became the secretary of one of the senior managers. Spontaneously she started experiencing new energy and passion when she had to organise meetings, make appointments and deal with people on different levels. It was a different environment and gradually she shed the feeling of stupidity – other skills, other criteria, a different kind of knowledge and encouragement now became important. For the first time in her life Priscilla started feeling clever and developed self-confidence which led to new visions. After negotiating with the bank she eventually obtained a loan which enabled her to start her own business – she offered a service as a consultant, planning and organising conferences, workshops, speakers and training for companies and organisations.

After four years in the business, her staff had grown to 40 members and she was managing one of the most successful firms in this field, with excellent prospects for the future. So we see that 'school stupid' did not make Priscilla 'life stupid', and neither did it label her professionally or financially stupid.

Narrative

Robert Maila

Robert grew up in one of the townships and because of the depressing economic circumstances of his environment there was very little opportunity to study. He lived in a small, two-roomed house with his parents, three brothers and a sister.

Later his grandmother also moved in with them. In the afternoons Robert usually had to work in and around the house, and there was no time for schoolwork. At school he simply drifted from one grade to the next, until he left school at the end of the seventh grade. He was 15 years old then and the only job he could find, after more than two months of job-hunting, was at a supermarket where he had to help unload fruit and vegetables from delivery trucks and pack them onto the shelves. He found the work boring, but enjoyed handling the vegetables and fruit. Very soon he knew how to grade the produce and the few times he had to deal with the customers directly, he could give them good advice on the quality of the fresh produce.

After a few years he got a job at the market where he had to deal directly with dispatching the fresh produce. It did not take him long to acquire the skills of this trade, and eventually he decided to start his own fresh-produce business. The first two stands on which he displayed his fruit and vegetables were erected at a busy taxi-rank and bus-stop. It was an instant success. Within the first month Robert doubled his stock, and also erected stands in other strategic places. After the first year he had 30 vendors and his business was flourishing. Robert not only became financially successful, but his job also filled him with great passion and joy. To him it also meant rediscovering *clever* qualities which had always been present, but needed to be unleashed through a combination of factors.

Narrative

Hennie Lehman

Hennie always performed very well at school. He was a dedicated student who scored top marks in the natural sciences. Traditionally, students who did well at these subjects were regarded as clever, and Hennie's parents were of the same opinion. They believed he had to do a BSc degree because of the straight A's he was scoring in Mathematics and Science. It was a matter of course that *clever* students ought to obtain a BSc degree and Hennie obliged by studying mechanical engineering and obtained his degree in the minimum time. He started working for a big iron and steel company.

After working for this company for nine years, and in spite of regular promotions, he became more and more disgruntled with his job. For the first time he admitted to himself that his studies and choice of career had been based solely on scholastic and academic achievements in specific subjects – those things that really gave him joy and filled him with passion were never even considered. At school and university he had served on various committees where he excelled at organising and planning social functions and gatherings. He often hosted these functions.

At the age of 33 Hennie decided to take the plunge which would enable him to combine his expertise with his preferences. He obtained a post as area manager of a company that supplied motor spares to various sales outlets. Here he could combine his formal qualifications with social and organisational skills and at last he could do what he both enjoyed and excelled at. After two years in this new post, Hennie was promoted to national manager and is experiencing ongoing passion for his work.

Hennie is a classical example of the dated and misplaced preconceived conceptions of clever and stupid. Obviously his studies had not been in vain, but the label attached exclusively to this particular field was not only a misrepresentation of the concepts clever and stupid, but it also led to conditioned thinking. Methods employed to ensure that only the academic 'elite' were selected for these courses resulted in the following:

• excellent achievements by individuals and small groups

- a high percentage became so focused on science that they no longer saw the 'big picture' – they could not see the wood for the trees
- in a certain sense students allowed themselves to be almost forced into these courses because it was expected of them, and then later they became frustrated and discontented (like Hennie)
- many other potential achievers in the sciences were not given the opportunity to realise this potential because of external circumstances like inferior education (accompanied by the negative self-esteem resulting from this) and were consequently 'disqualified' in the early stages

In all three cases discussed here, moments and times of stupid and clever were experienced. Naturally it would be possible to identify genetic factors which could explain aspects of clever and stupid. Without however, going into the age-old debate on heredity versus environment, it is essential to review the definitions which have prevailed with regard to intelligence and non-intelligence. (Certain aspects of these definitions were discussed at the beginning of the chapter.)

- A score of 130+ in the standard intelligence test puts you in the clever category and below 100 in the lower-than-average to stupid category (-85).
- Scoring A's in tests, examinations and other forms of testing is regarded as a sure sign of cleverness.
- Exceptional achievement in mathematics and the natural sciences is an indisputable sign of being clever (and in comparison a poor performance in other subjects does not count).
- Poor performance in certain subjects, or giving up on certain subjects/courses (especially mathematics) is a strong indication of stupidity.

These broad outlines can be regarded as generalisations, that is true, but our research over fifteen years has clearly shown that the above-mentioned views are realistic and standard, and experienced as such by the average person. It is also true that as times change, there is consistent dynamic change in the demands made on us:

- focus on universal human rights
- radical changes in the business environment, from:
  - multi-levelled to flatter organisations
  - autocracy to interactive management
  - the-boss-knows-everything to everyone-has-a-say
  - immediate environments to global markets
  - clumsiness to an essential suppleness
  - idling to supersonic communication
    (add at least 30 paradigm shifts to these)
- revolutionary changes with regard to the nature, contents and aims/objectives of education
- environmental consciousness which leads to the forming of power blocks and new bargaining strategies
- computer networking and technological innovation which affect the essence of every industry
- re-evaluating the effect of super powers
- continual demands of 21st century projections on the visions of each individual and organisation.
  (See if you can indicate another 10 paradigm shifts which have occurred in your lifetime during recent years.)

Thus we see that if we do not keep up, in spite of the radical changes in circumstances, environments and needs, and persist in clinging to narrow-minded and obsolete definitions of the requirements for achievement, we shall not only cut ourselves off from opportunities and achievements, but society in general will be impoverished.

This book is an attempt at shedding light on human gifts and abilities within the context of today and hopefully also that of tomorrow. It wishes to re-awaken the hope and dream inside of you, so that you can keep on rediscovering *your* clever. Allow your thinking to remain open and fresh while you travel through the different chapters. The more receptive you are – and this is your own decision – the more this creative journey will mean to you personally.

> If we all did the things we are capable of doing, we would literally astound ourselves.
> **– Thomas A Edison –**

Getting to grips with yourself

Chapter 2

Projections regarding the type of professions which would dominate the initial stages of the 21st century, indicate that about 80 % of these do not even exist yet. This means that an ongoing flow of new insights, skills and constant renewal of knowledge must be incorporated in our thinking, if we are to survive and prosper.

Yesterday's *clever* might not be today or tomorrow's *clever* and the constant rediscovery of latent creative skills should not be left to chance. This means continually exploring and developing our creative skills so that we can cope with the explosive change taking place around us at a pace which will never slow down again. We all have the potential to be courageous and passionate and to undertake the *Creative Journey*.

Defining creativity

There are more than 400 definitions of creativity and yet not a single one really captures the wonder of this amazing concept. Because creativity is an experience, a new attitude toward one's personal life, business, organisation, one's world, it is almost impossible to fence in this world.

 The closest one can get to a definition, would be to say: Creativity is looking at the world with a fresh pair of eyes. Creativity is a lifestyle – it is the way you think, the way you dream, it is the way you do things. It is

- **going beyond**
- **spreading your wings**
- **finding 200 ways of saying, "Well done!"**

- **digging deeper**
- **wanting to know**
- **singing in your own key**
- **never saying never**
- **shaking hands with the future**

(According to Paul Torrance these are explanations children supplied when asked to define creativity.)

The primary skills

The truth about creativity and its value is this: it is the difference between the ordinary and the mediocre; between success and excellence. It is a skill that opens up new worlds – worlds you merely dreamt about.

Creativity is not a fixed hereditary characteristic (unlike IQ, that feared and revered label which categorised us so rigidly as clever or stupid!). It is in fact an ability which, if nurtured, will grow and flourish. You **can** be creative! You **can** become the thinker you have never been before! You **can** be clever!

Truly creative people generally possess a few (or many) of the following characteristics:

- They *recognise* and are *aware* of problems. They are able to *define* problems and are committed to deal with them. When confronted with a problem they are able to see it in a wider context, *open it up*, and *redefine* it in such a way that sub-problems, which are more manageable, can be identified and solved.

- In their thinking they are able to get away from the *obvious* and *commonplace*, to *generate* statistically *rare*, *original* ideas.

- In spite of the great many possible alternative solutions, they are able to *focus on* the *important* and *essential*. This means they *synthesise,* at the same time *discarding* incorrect or irrelevant information, unfavourable facts or solutions; they redefine ideas, establish priorities, and select a *single idea* or problem as being the *dominant* one.

• Having chosen an alternative, they are able to work out the details of *implementing* their great idea (as well as *elaborating* on these details). This is the only way in which this idea will be of value and gain acceptance.

• When faced with an unsolved problem they do not prematurely jump to the same dull and mundane conclusions. They are able to *delay decision-making* long enough for the mind to take the necessary mental leaps if it is to produce a truly *original solution*.

Fluency (Generating ideas)

The ability to generate more ideas and alternatives is an essential prerequisite to innovative and successful problem solving. The more alternatives a person/group produces, the more viable the ideas and solutions are likely to be, and the greater the likelihood of successful problem solving.

Any parent, teacher or organisation is heading for disaster if there are only a few alternatives available to them. In order to discipline, educate, motivate, sell, plan, organise and manage effectively it is essential to produce and keep on producing more and better ideas.

How fluent are *you?*

Activity

You can drink a cold drink through a straw. To what other uses could you put a straw? (Work on this for 3 minutes.)

In how many ways can you compliment someone on a job well done? (Work for 3 minutes)

Originality

Although fluency increases the possibility of producing original ideas, there is no guarantee that this will occur. There is usually a relatively high correlation between fluency and originality in creativity tests – normally around 0,6. However, originality testing usually predicts creative behaviour more accurately than fluency testing does.

Established habits often restrict the way we look at things and we become accustomed to conformity and the conventional. The original thinker is comfortable with being different; this is the way in which a constant stream of original ideas is produced. In order to generate ideas that make an impact, to take mental leaps, we need to look beyond the ordinary.

There cannot be real growth if we remain stuck in the rut of merely *re*producing – it is 'new thinking' which results in solutions, cures, and creates a worthwhile future.

To be more original you need to

- look beyond the ordinary
- move on – from reproducing to producing
- be a new and exciting thinker and doer.

 Obstacles which block the way to

originality:

❑ **Habit, convention and conformity**
Habit often blocks unconventional ways of looking at things. For example, when working on the **activities** for fluency, some ideas probably occurred to you that you did not write down or mention. As we grow up our minds become accustomed to conformity and consequently we often find ourselves hesitant and timid about expressing thoughts that are unique or strange.

❑ **Ideas often rejected**
You can most probably think of one or more ideas that, for some reason, you rejected while you were busy with the previous activities. If you go back through your complete chain of mental processes you will almost certainly find that you thought of ideas that did not seem sensible or important enough to mention or consider at the time.

❑ **Anxiety about ideas**
Most of us are not comfortable with expressing our ideas. This often prevents us from mentioning all the things we think of, or we don't even consider them. In order to generate plenty of ideas, we must allow ourselves to look beyond the conventional ways of observing situations.

❑ Rash judgment

When novel ideas originate they often contain an element of foolishness at first. It is this element of foolishness in the original idea which often serves as an important building-block towards problem solving. In other words, unconventional ideas – even if they seem ridiculous at first – can often be shaped and refined into new and useful solutions. So it is important to avoid premature and harsh judgment of your own ideas, and those of others, even though at first they might seem stupid or even bizarre.

In the early stages of generating new ideas, it is necessary that imagination takes priority over judgment.

How original are you?

Plan a 'humour room' for a company where employees can get rid of their frustrations. Use different themes that take everybody's taste into account. (Work for 30 minutes.)

_____

_____

_____

_____

_____

How can you create opportunities which would allow everybody in the company/home/school to come up with creative ideas? (Work for 15 minutes.)

_____

_____

_____

_____

Choose an original metaphor to symbolise the qualities of your company/school/club. Explain. (Think beyond the usual, for example a dove symbolising peace, a lion strength, etc.)

Focus on the essence

Many people are overwhelmed by the "mess" they uncover when unravelling a problem, or by the many alternatives they are confronted with. Consequently they either freeze and come to a standstill, or deal with the less important problem, or choose an obvious and inferior solution that does not solve the real problem. They lose sight of what is important or essential and fail to focus on the essence.

Focusing on the essence means:

- discarding faulty and irrelevant information
- cutting out facts and solutions which will serve no purpose
- refining ideas
- establishing priorities
- allowing a single problem or idea to become dominant.

How good are you at focusing on the essence?

Write titles for each of the following drawings:

(a)

Title:_____

(b)

Title:_____

(c)

Title:_____

 You are advertising a new sweet.

Write an advertisement for a magazine, taking into account the following:

- Your target group is young children.
- Health is important to your company.
- The most innovative idea is that the wrapper can also be eaten.

_____

_____

_____

_____

_____

_____

Elaboration

It is not enough to merely create or invent something, to think up a good story, or a great idea for solving a future problem. A detailed elaboration is necessary – of the idea, its implementation, its value and relation to other ideas if it is to be sold and the product accepted.

Yet it is possible to get carried away and overdo this elaboration to such an extent that people are overwhelmed by detail, or that it becomes far too expensive. Fluency, flexibility and originality are sacrificed if elaboration becomes too extravagant. On the other hand, the ability to elaborate, to work out and implement plans and sell solutions is important and must be practised.

The major uses of elaboration are:

- to produce anything creative that can be recognised, valued and used;
- to plan something new or innovative – what, who, when, where, how, how much time will it take, how much will it cost?
- to break down resistance to new ideas.

How good are you at elaborating?

You have been asked to organise an outing for your company/ school/club. Draw up a questionnaire you can circulate to get some idea of what most of the employees/members would enjoy.

Remain open – guard against a closure of thinking!

When faced with unfinished or unsolved problems, almost every-one tends to jump to some conclusions immediately. Frequently this jump is made prematurely – before the person has taken the time to understand the problem, consider important factors involved and think of alternative solutions.

This impulsive behaviour usually results in solutions which lack originality and freshness. Such solutions are not only dull and unimaginative, they also frequently make matters worse.

In the creative process there must be a willingness to permit one thing to lead to another, a readiness to break away from the beaten track or to escape the mould, an openness to reach out, to relate and connect.

How open is your mind/thinking?

Activity

Write down all the similarities you can think of between:
– a lighthouse and a cat:

_____

_____

_____

_____

_____

– a postage stamp and an ice lolly:

_____

_____

_____

_____

_____

_____

Activity Think of a person you really do not like. Write down the reasons why you dislike this person. Now, with an open mind, write down this person's positive qualities. Keep your mind open, and do not revert to negative thinking.

Negative thoughts:

● _____

● _____

● _____

● _____

● _____

● _____

Positive qualities:

● _____

● _____

● _____

● _____

● _____

● _____

Creating your own vision and plans of action

You chose to start out on your journey of discovery. At this stage you need to take a hard look at yourself, and then plan the journey which lies ahead. Become involved in your own destiny – it can be exciting!

Complete the following work sheet. Fill in three creative accomplishments you can recall from your recent past under each category. Then fill in five creative accomplishments you would *like to achieve* in the immediate future.

Job/Studies

1._____

2._____

3._____

1._____

2._____

3._____

4._____

5._____

Family

1._____

2._____

3._____

1._____

2._____

3._____

4._____

5._____

Attitude/Point of View

1._____

2._____

3._____

1._____

2._____

3._____

4._____

5._____

Our research shows that a small percentage of people excel at the application of all the primary creative skills, while those who excel at only one or two of these skills outnumber them by far. You might feel more comfortable as an elaborator, rather than a creator of ideas, or vice versa. (In most instances this has to do with personal preferences.) A final product which is any good needs the input of both the elaborator and the one who generated the idea – and this is fundamental to understanding your own cleverness. Sometimes the cleverness of one person is not sufficient, and more is needed for ultimate success. It may happen that you develop this other skill, but at times it will be necessary to join hands with someone else so that together you possess the qualities that are necessary to achieve your goals.

In almost every field of human achievement, creativity is usually the distinguishing characteristic of the truly eminent. The possession of high intelligence, special talent and high technical skills is not enough to produce outstanding achievement.
– Paul Torrance (1959)

Say proudly, "I did this myself."

Chapter 3

James Allen writes that a person's mind may be likened to a garden which is either intelligently cultivated or allowed to run wild. But whether cultivated or neglected, it must and will produce *something*. If you do nothing about that garden, if you sow no seeds, useless weeds will take over and steadily destroy the garden. In this chapter we focus on closed and open thinking, before we embark on our whole brain journey. Closing the mind is a deliberate choice. When it starts happening spontaneously, a conditioned thinking mode has manifested.

 In his book, *The Different Drum*, M. Scott Peck tells a story called The Rabbi's Gift. In this story the abbot of a dying Christian order consisting of only five monks (all of them over seventy), pays a visit to an old rabbi who is stopping over at a place near the order's dilapidated house.

They commiserate with each other over the lack of religious fervour in the world. As they embrace, the abbot asks the rabbi if there is any advice he can give him to take back to the monks and which will help them save this dying Christian order. The rabbi replies, "I have no advice to give. The only thing I can tell you is that one of you is the Messiah."

When the abbot reports this to the monks they all start wondering about the others and about themselves and begin to treat themselves and one another as if each one is the Messiah. People who happen to be in the vicinity of the monastery are attracted by the exceptional love, respect and caring they observe and experience there. More and more people come to visit and to pray. A stream of young men start joining the order and it begins to grow and flourish. Not only

do people from this region start talking about this order, but it also becomes an extraordinary example of devotion and religious energy to people all over the world.

This story is a perfect example of the effect of closed thinking versus the creative miracles which are possible when you open up your way of thinking and start to experience empowerment in its true sense. Once the monks started moving beyond their old thinking patterns based on logic and rigidity, a new consciousness and vitality emerged. It led to a new kind of awakening, a Messiah awakening. And this ongoing discovery of creative dimensions is a never-ending process. Their locked-in power and dead energy are replaced by liberation and empowerment. They discover that once they transform themselves, they can transform the world in spite of their age (all of them over seventy) and in spite of their waning past.

Rid yourself of closed thinking

If we believe that excellence is a moving target we must accept that it remains a constant quest. If we convince ourselves that we have attained excellence, we have boxed in and set limits to something that defies all limits. The search requires an open state of mind, "a rage against the dying of the light". Merely *knowing* what to *do* is not enough. You must also *do* what you *know*.

In Chapter 1 we stated that the only thing you are able to change is your thinking. The monks also discovered this truth: when they changed their way of thinking they started changing the world. So the promise this holds is that every person is able to access joy and freedom even in the most depressing circumstances. Fact is that you think yourself into a state of depression, unhappiness and negativity; and, conversely, you can think yourself out of that state as well.

Negativity has never accomplished anything

I believe that we have tolerated and accommodated negativity far too long, instead of putting an end to it. No one is born with negative attitudes and therefore it is an acquired and unnatural process which is brought upon us by a number of factors, such as:

- weak support systems as a child (and as an adult)
- deliberately and/or subconsciously placing limitations on your innate abilities
- putting yourself down
- being belittled by others
- poor performance at school (or in particular subjects)
- the wrong career choices
- wrong and unsuccessful relationships
- external crises
- exclusion
- dramatic change
- not fulfilling your aspirations
- no future vision
- lack of feedback
- poverty
- environment and culture
- illness

Activity

(This list is not complete and you could add factors which cause negativity in you.)

_____

_____

_____

_____

_____

_____

The above-mentioned factors affect you to the extent that you start convincing yourself you cannot get what you want. You start undermining your own dreams and aspirations and eventually also the desires and objectives of your family and your organisation. This negativity then spreads and starts affecting people and processes at every level. The negativity the individual experiences about himself then also spills over onto his family or his club or the organisation where he is employed. Most of his or her time is spent on:

- judging others
- gossip
- criticising people/ideas/policies
- complaining (and this becomes a way of life)
- sarcastic remarks
- nit-picking
- rebelling against authority
- self-pity
- procrastinating
- sabotaging self (or others)
- avoiding people or situations
- pursuing the wrong things
- intolerance
- abusing others
- being spiteful
- living yesterday over and over again

Once this negativity starts bombarding your thinking, the latter is in danger of being conditioned and boxed in. And once you start responding to specific knowledge, experiences, people, ideas and change in a conditioned and predictable way, the process could intensify to such a degree that you think negatively about everything. You become a slave to your own thinking, and this often makes you irrational, defensive and fills you with resentment. You process your thinking from memory only, with the result that you become predictable and very often also inferior and redundant.

Closed mind excuses

The following excuses were listed over a period of time, and compiled from the negative responses of people when confronted with change and transformation. Read through the list and add your own experiences of closed-mind responses.

Which responses do you think are typical of you?

We'll discuss it later
We've tried that before
Our place is different
It's too expensive
That's not my job
It's too radical a change
They're too busy to do that
We are too busy
Not enough support
The staff will never buy it
It's against company policy
The unions will complain
This is running up our overheads
We don't have the authority
Get real
This is not our problem
I don't like the idea
You're right, but …
You're way ahead of your time
We're not ready for that
We didn't budget for this
Are you crazy?
Good thought, but not practical
Let's think about this again
We'll be the laughing stock of…

You are way out of line, man
Where did you dig this up?
We did all right without it
Where is the proof?
Let's just leave it at that for the time being
Let's form a committee
I don't see the connection
It won't work in our plant/office
They would never go for it
Let's all sleep on it
It can't be done
It's too much trouble to change
The project won't pay for itself
I know someone who tried it
It's impossible
We've always done it this way
Top management won't buy it
We'd lose money in the long run
Don't rock the boat
That's what we can expect from the staff
Has anyone else ever tried it?
Let's not go into the matter
Stop dreaming – wake up
This won't work in our organisation
This looks a lot like an ivory tower
It's too much work

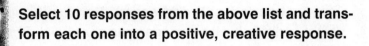

Activity

Select 10 responses from the above list and transform each one into a positive, creative response.

Closed Example: You're right, but ...	Open Example: You're right, and ...
	.

The anti-negativity programme

Anne was walking down the street. She was down-hearted and depressed. Her family was being difficult. Her manager was a problem. She thought this was going to be just another miserable day. Then she walked into a supermarket to buy groceries. At the front entrance she saw a stand displaying the most beautiful flowers. On the spur of the moment she went over, took a bunch of red and pink roses and put it into her basket. She smiled, her face lit up and she noticed a smiling mother and child also looking at the flowers. Suddenly she experienced a shift in thinking and she began to notice the laughter and energy of the people around her; maybe her family was not so difficult after all and maybe her boss was not that bad.

Anne walked out of the supermarket in a completely different frame of mind. Her circumstances had not changed, but her negative thinking had – it had become positive. Thus her circumstances did not control her any more.

The negative (closed) Anne:	The positive (open) Anne:
• My family members are difficult	• My family members are characters
• My manager causes problems	• My manager poses a challenge
• This is just another dreary day	• Every day is what I make of it

Many famous people who brought about permanent change in communities, organisations, businesses and even in their countries, first had to break free from the *closed Anne syndrome* in order to work miracles.

- **Edison and Einstein are well-known examples of miracle-workers who were told by their teachers that they had no hope of succeeding.**
- **Football experts told Vince Lombardi that he lacked know-ledge of football and that he could not motivate people – he became one of the most successful football coaches.**
- **Tony Factor, who became a very successful South African business leader, left school at a very early age because of a so-called inability to perform at school.**
- **Beethoven's teacher told him he was a hopeless composer.**

- Walt Disney, universal example of a creative spirit, became internationally famous as a creative genius – yet he was fired by a newspaper because he lacked ideas.
- The great Enrico Caruso was told by his teacher that he should give up singing; his efforts were in vain because he did not have a singing voice.

If we look around us we could keep on adding to this list indefinitely. If any of the above-mentioned people had closed their thinking and believed that they were stupid we would not have known a Beethoven or a Disney – and this planet would have been so much the poorer for it.

You cannot afford to close your thinking every time you are faced with conflict, problems or rejection. It is then that the thinking pattern of "I don't feel good about myself", and "It's not for me" takes over and tears you apart.

Study the following V-graph which explains the difference in (and also different consequences of) open and closed thinking.

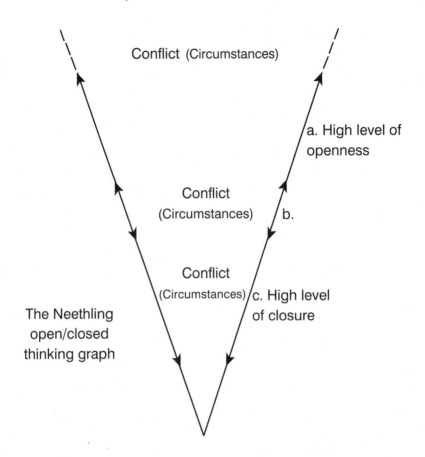

The Neethling open/closed thinking graph

Explanation of the graph

1. A person at **point b** on the graph is wavering somewhere between closed and open thinking and could respond in an open or closed way in any given circumstances (hence the arrows pointing up and down).

2. A person at **point a** shows a very high degree of openness and will almost invariably respond in an open way to any given conflict or problem. (The arrows pointing upwards and the dotted lines going up have no limits because open thinking has no limits.)

3. A person at **point c** shows a very high degree of closure and will almost always close up and respond negatively to any given challenge or change (the downward arrows suggest this closure which will result in yesterday's thinking/conditioned thinking).

Where are you on this graph?

There is no such thing as thinking which is so permanently closed that it cannot open up again. Anyone – it does not matter where you find yourself on this graph today – can choose to change negative thinking. Very often we cannot change particular circumstances, but we can change the way we think about those circumstances. The more we put our open thinking into practice, the better the chances of becoming an open, positive thinker – not sporadically but permanently. One could not wish for anything more rewarding than the joy, the energy, the peace, the freedom and creativity that come with this state of mind.

The 22-day open thinking programme

If you follow this programme for the next 22 days the chances of changing your negative attitude are excellent. It is recommended that your family members and colleagues join in and that group members support one another. It is also recommended that you make copies of the example on the next page so that you can keep your own 22-day diary which you can take with you wherever you go.

Rules of the programme

1. For the next 22 days write down in column 1 of the chart every negative thought that enters your mind.
2. Immediately change that thought (or feeling) into positive ideas (as many as you can think of) and write these down in column 2.
3. Write down the feeling you experience when transforming negativity into creative solutions in column 3.

Declare war on negativity so that your permanent state of mind becomes one of solution-thinking and not problem-thinking.

Day —		
Negative thoughts	**Positive thoughts**	**Feeling**
1.		
2.		
3.		
4.		
5.		
6.		
7.		

Resisting negative thinking is a clever choice

Once you have said goodbye to negative thinking you need never return to it – the choice is yours. An open mind sees more and better opportunities and soars with the eagles. So before you move on to the next chapter, read this chapter once more. The journey from now on will be so much more fun and exciting if you leave your conditioned thinking behind. On this earth we only live once, but if we live right, once is enough.

Promod Batra writes as follows about the law of success:

If you think you are beaten, you are;
If you think you dare not, you don't;
If you'd like to win, but you think you can't
It is almost certain you won't.

If you think you'll lose you've lost.
Success begins with a person's will
It's all in the state of mind.
If you think you're outclassed, you are.
You've got to be sure of yourself before
You can ever win a prize.
Life's battles don't always go
To the stronger or faster man;
But sooner or later the man who wins
Is the man who thinks he can!

Being clever starts with:
- thinking you are clever
- resisting stupid thoughts
- believing that you are clever
- demonstrating that you are clever.

Everything can be taken from a man but one thing: the last of the human freedoms — to choose one's attitude in any given set of circumstances, to choose one's own way.
   – Victor Frankl, Auschwitz prisoner and author of *Man's search for meaning* –

Where it all begins ?

Chapter 4

It is the mind that maketh good or ill, that maketh wretched or happy, rich or poor.
– Edmund Spenser –

Someone once said you are the master of your thoughts, the moulder of your character, and the maker and shaper of your conditions and destiny. In the following chapters we focus on the foundations of psychological functioning – your mind, your thinking and your consciousness. Once you understand that insight and 'ahas' are always available, it becomes so much easier to venture outside the confines of your conditioned ways of thinking. You are then able to release yourself from the negative realities which have held you captive for so long. Understanding left/right brain thinking and whole brain functioning will bring about new perspectives resulting in creative solutions and breakthroughs. Once you start realising that thinking is the starting point, you can break the cycle of mediocrity and it will begin to dawn on you that you are not stupid or at best, average.

 ## Left and right brain

In *Creative People can perform Miracles* (Kobus Neethling, Carpe Diem Books Vanderbijlpark) I explain left or right brain functioning as follows:

In 1981 a neuro-surgeon, Robert Sperry, was award-ed the Nobel Prize for his research on the split-brain theory. This theory proved that a human being tends to use one part of the brain more than the other, and that this tendency strongly influences the person's physical and mental abilities, his personality, his approach to people and things and his ability to solve problems.

The research also clearly indicated why one person is, for instance, excellent at working with numbers but feels uncom-fortable in a group situation, and why another person gene-rates wonderful ideas but finds it impossible to structure and act upon them.

This is the case not only with individuals, but it is also found in any group, organisation or company. It can for exam-ple, happen in an organisation that the work and culture focus is rooted in exclusively left brain preference. If the employees and the mission of the company also show left brain preferen-ces there should be complete harmony and a uniformity of vision.

If, however, and this is usually the case, the brain preferen-ces of people who work there vary, then this factor will have to be taken into account in all facets of the organisation – its management and mission, its goals and culture. Dynamic managers and entrepreneurs who excel, virtually always de-monstrate throughout that they are capable of using both sides of the brain when circumstances demand it.

Parents and teachers will be surprised at the success they achieve, and the joy they experience when they accept and acknowledge that there are different brain preferences, and learn how to determine the specific preferences of their chil-dren. It often happens that one child in a family has a logical, organised and systematic way of thinking, while another is disorganised; a dreamer who couldn't be bothered with detail. It can then happen that the parents wrongfully force one child to give up his brain preference (possibly to become more like the rest of them). This is wrong. Instead, his brain preference should be boosted, while, at the same time, he is made aware of the existence of other brain preferences (in the world, but also in his own home). He should be taught to hold his own in any environment without sacrificing his own preference. In this way the necessary understanding, attitude and skills are developed not only in the individual, but also in relation to the rest of the world around him.

A few concepts

Balling your fists with the thumbs pointing towards your body, gives an indication of how large your brain is. There is also another similarity between the fist and the brain ... the knuckles, folds and veins look like the uneven surface of the *neo-cortex* (the outer layer of the brain). The more folds and uneven surfaces indicated on the *neo-cortex*, the more information is stored by the brain. A new-born baby's brain is, for example, completely smooth as no learning or storing of information has taken place yet.

When referring to the brain and intelligence, the term 'grey matter' is often used. This term is correct up to a point. In reality the left brain has more grey matter in relation to white matter than the right brain. The grey matter of the left brain is an indication of how many organised facts a person has mastered, while the white matter of the right brain processes a large variety of visual, sensory and emotional material. It is this right brain activity which generally leads to intuition – the gut-feel approach.

References to the dual nature of the brain are found in early manuscripts. The observers of human behaviour could at the time however, give no explanation for this so-called dualism. A psychological basis for this phenomenon was identified for the first time in the nineteen sixties.

In their treatment of and research on epileptic patients Roger Sperry and Michael Gazzaniga discovered that the *corpus callosum*, the connecting channel between the left and right brain, is responsible for the essential communication between the two parts. As some of the patients were in the process of dying as a result of the advanced nature of their illness, researchers decided to sever the channel between the two parts of the brain. The effect was immediate – the occurrence of epileptic fits was brought down to a controllable level.

It then became possible to test each of the hemispheres separately. The results as set out in the following diagrams, indicate that each hemisphere absorbs information in a different way, and that one is unaware of the other's manner of learning or processing of information.

Research on the two hemispheres of the brain concluded that each hemisphere deals with information in a different way.

 The left brain

Research shows that left brain thinking is, amongst others:
- analytical
- exact
- logical
- detailed
- structured
- verbal
- rational
- concrete
- linear
- technical

- fact based
- organised
- planned
- autocratic
- mathematical

(The left brain controls the right side of the body.)

The right brain

Processes controlled by the right hemisphere, include:
- intuition
- non-linear thinking
- space
- holism
- the non-verbal
- feeling
- music
- expressiveness
- interaction
- visualising
- insight
- gut-feeling
(The right brain controls the left side of the body.)

Do you understand which processes are associated with the two hemispheres of the brain?

Design an office that somebody with left brain preferences would like to work in.

Now design an office that somebody with right brain preferences would like to work in.

Left brain office

Right brain office

Left brain	Right brain
8:00	8:00 Aah!
9:00 Dentist	9:00
10:00	10:00
11:00	11:00 Remember
12:00	12:00
13:00 Lunch - Susan	13:00
14:00	14:00
15:00	15:00
16:00 Phone - John	16:00 Brother
17:00	17:00 ask - Tuckshop
18:00	18:00 Clothing
19:00 PTA Meeting	19:00 Fees!

Left and right brain creativity

Traditionally, right brain dominant people have been labelled creative and left brain dominant people regarded as logical and rigid. Today we realise that people with a right brain thinking preference as well as those with a left brain thinking preference can think and act creatively. We all have a unique way of dealing with our creativity.

You might not even be aware of the fact that you have the ability to think creatively. Fact is, we are faced with challenges every day – and sometimes we deal with them by doing something new, something different, even though it does not seem so unique at the time.

You might have discovered a way of making a boring task more enjoyable, or you may have started handling somebody in a different way, with good results. Or perhaps you modified a recipe, a road map or instruction manual to serve your purpose better. Without realising it, you have most probably been creative quite often – in your own unique way.

A few facts to remember about yourself, your brain and creativity:

- You *can* be creative.
- Creativity implies whole brain thinking.
- You have to do something about your creativity – get started.
- Creativity and negativity do not go together.
- Creativity can be taught and learned.
- Creativity is not necessarily a result of breakthrough thinking – look around you and change what needs to be changed.
- Creativity is strongly influenced by culture, environment and space.
- Creativity is more a matter of breaking down barriers and coping with life than acquiring skills and techniques.

Do you think you have ever been creative in your thinking?

 Think of a situation (quite recently or long ago) in which you were confronted with a challenge and had to make use of your creative abilities to meet it. It need not necessarily be a very meaningful experience.

Now think of a situation which you feel you did not handle very well. How could you have handled it differently for better results?

 # Coping Creatively

The challenge

Your creativity is unique. You possess your own brand of creativity which means you perceive problems, situations and people in a specific way and thus you will handle situations and people in your own unique way.

Now think back to some of your creative experiences – noteworthy ones, or even ones that seem comparatively unimportant. Do not force your mind into a certain direction, rather allow your memories to flow freely from one experience to another. Do this for some time, trying to remember as many different creative experiences as possible. Now see if one experience tends to stick in your mind longer than others. Focus on this one, relive it. Try to recall all the relevant facts, how you handled this experience, how you felt and what the outcome was.

 Now answer the following questions:

● **Which experience stands out in your mind? Try to put the challenge it presented into words.**

_____

_____

- How did the challenge of the situation make you feel? Give your positive and negative reactions.

_____

_____

- Where did this challenge occur?

_____

_____

- What was the first idea that came to mind in your attempt to solve your problem and meet this particular challenge?

_____

_____

- How many ideas did you discard before you decided on a final course of action?

_____

_____

- How did you arrive at the solution and how did you feel then?

_____

_____

- Did you implement your idea?

_____

_____

- Who was influenced? What was influenced? What then?

_____

_____

The tools

In order to be successful you need to use certain essential tools during the creative process. If you analyse the creative experiences you have just recalled, you will probably find that you used most of these tools.

❑ Believing in your creativity

Many of us grew up quite unaware of this inner strength we all possess. It is a human trait to build up resistance to anything new, even if it is something positive. Because of past failures, we lose faith in our ability to cope with problems and tricky situations in a creative way.

To be truly creative, we need to believe first of all that we can be innovative. This gives us courage to generate new ideas, and so our own unique creativity becomes evident. Faith in our own creative abilities becomes the fertile soil necessary for growth.

Believing that you are creative does not mean knowing you are always right. What it does mean is that failure is not the end of the road. It means you will travel other roads before you discover the one which leads to success.

❑ Avoiding negative thinking

If you prejudge people and situations, chances are that you will not be able to open up yourself to the creative experience. It is only when we refrain from judging others and ourselves (for what we can and cannot do; should or should not do) that we can reach our creative potential.

Activity

How negative do you think you are?

Write a few lines on how you perceive your own level of negativity.

_____

_____

_____

_____

_____

❏ **Asking the right questions**

Creativity is looking at the world with a fresh pair of eyes. It is asking new questions which will give new perspective on the situation.

What do you know about the present challenge? Who is involved? Who will be affected by the decisions? What are the hidden possibilities? What feelings (your own, or those of others) are involved? How did you handle a similar situation in the past? How many possibilities are there?

Asking new questions is a way of keeping your mind open – long enough to come up with the creative solution that will solve the problem.

In the next chapter I hope to bring you closer to the answer of this question by explaining your thinking preferences – the very essence of who you really are.

The most important thing is this: To be able at any moment to sacrifice what we are for what we could become.

– Charles du Bois –

Clever is
understanding
whole brain
functioning

Chapter 5

If you want to take an active part in redesigning your life you have to examine the rules and values which have governed your life up to now and decide if they are still meaningful today. Start by making a few crucial decisions now – not tomorrow. (Maybe these rules and values were not even meaningful yesterday or the day before!)

In this chapter we show you how to start the whole brain process. An understanding of this process can help you to rediscover thinking and clarify why you like to do certain things and why others frustrate and irritate you.

The Neethling Brain Instrument, a computer programme designed to determine your thinking preferences, will form the basis of our discussion on whole brain understanding.

This programme was developed after extensive international research since 1980 on left/right brain functioning. More than 200 000 adults and children from a number of countries have been profiled by means of the Neethling Brain Instrument (NBI). The results of research on the NBI have been very significant and ongoing research at a number of universities and institutes remains an essential part of whole brain science.

The Neethling Brain Instrument

The instrument consists of two programmes (one for children between the ages of approximately 11 to 17 years, and one for adults).

The programme is not a test and there are no right or wrong answers, good or poor responses (the final score of each participant totals 300), but each profile has definite situational implications. The Neethling Brain Profile measures the preferences an individual might have for performing certain tasks or mastering certain skills – it does not measure his/her abilities or skills.

The brain profile gives an indication of a person's brain preferences. They indicate how:

- comfortable (content) you are/should be in a certain career
- you act towards other people
- you do business
- you communicate
- you learn
- you teach
- you solve problems
- you make decisions, etc.

It is essential to understand your preferences before deciding to change, to shift paradigms or to develop particular skills.

Some of the fields in which the Neetling Brain Instrument has been put to good use, are:

❑ The business world

Knowledge of the brain preferences of, not only the people within an organisation, but also of clients and potential clients, can be successfully applied in marketing.

The profile of a job applicant would give a good indication of his/her suitability for a certain position.

A profile analysis of frustrated employees could result in shifts within the company, and it could happen that individuals are then placed in a department or position more suited to his/her preferences.

When an organisation wants to change (paradigm shifting), it is essential to determine the current thinking preferences of the company before deciding in which direction a shift should take place.

❑ Schools and other academic institutions

All academic institutions can obtain valuable information by identifying the brain preferences of both teachers and students.

Children with different brain preferences prefer to learn and study in different ways. Teachers ought to be aware of this and take note of the different brain preferences in a class and adapt their teaching style accordingly. This will result in teaching which is better understood and enjoyed more by all pupils.

Schools can make parents aware of different study methods and learning environments suited to a particular child's preference.

This information is invaluable when making career and subject choices.

❑ Human relations

In any relationship (marriage, family, friends, etc.), insight into your own brain preferences and those of others can prove to be a great help towards better understanding and co-operation.

People often misunderstand one another, because what might be perfectly logical to one person with a specific brain preference, might make no sense to another with a different brain preference.

When we understand the differences between people, it makes us more tolerant of each other.

❑ Personal growth

Although a lack of preference in a certain field does not impair your competency, it will not generate the same level of passion and motivation.

Becoming familiar with your own preferences and those of others, will make you more tolerant and less negative towards those who differ from you.

Living, playing and working together can become more mean-ingful and productive when different preferences start complementing one another. People will stop rejecting and avoiding one another as they find that their differences can stimulate growth and development.

 Profiling your brain

The Neethling Brain Instrument (NBI) consists of 30 questions. Remember, there are no right or wrong answers and no such thing as a good or a bad profile. Everyone scores a total of 300 points. The distribution of points over the four quadrants however, has important implications for the participant. Trained representatives can analyse these profiles and advise on subject and career choices, etc.

The following are examples of such profiles:

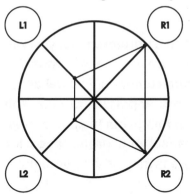

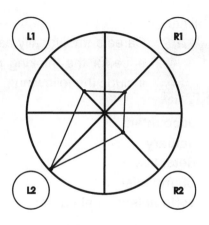

The L1-quadrant (upper left)

Key words

The thinking processes most commonly associated with the top left quadrant of the brain are the following:

- likes working with facts
- deals with facts/issues in a precise and exact way
- looks at problems in a logical and rational way
- likes working with numbers
- interested in technical aspects
- performance is important
- prefers to analyse facts

So if you are a person with strong L1 preferences, you will solve problems in a logical way, you are precise, will consider financial aspects, and not show much emotion. Factual accuracy and the evaluation of facts are important to you. You might not be interested in technical things but in spite of this, still be a strong L1 person, because your preferences for exactness and precision in other areas may be very dominant.

Careers

Careers traditionally associated with a strong preference for the thinking processes of the L1-quadrant include the following:

accountant
actuary
detective
pharmacist
various technical careers

surveyor
certain engineers
dentist
banker
computer scientist
scientist
surgeon
researcher
broker
pilot

Obviously there are other careers which can be added to this list. The essence is a preference for precision and/or for working with numbers or facts and/or logic, etcetera.

Going about your daily business

The way we conduct ourselves daily also depends on our brain preferences. Whether you are selling, shopping, communicating, driving a car or studying, it is your preferred mode of thinking that will make you think and act the way you do. Take as an example:

Buying a house
When buying a house the person with strong L1 preferences would probably go about it (act and think) in the following way: He or she:

- *insists on all available information*
- *regards cost, deposit, etc. as dominant factors throughout the transaction*
- *looks at the neatness, orderliness of the house and garden*
- *investigates the qualities of the house (pluses and minuses)*
- *makes constant comparisons with other houses (compares facts)*
- *does not allow feelings to cloud the real issues*

Am I clever or am I stupid?

Are you starting to understand the (left upper) L1-quadrant of the brain?

Do you think applicants for the following positions should have strong L1 preferences? Give reasons for your answers.

Insurance salesperson

_____

_____

Chemical engineer

_____

_____

Historian

_____

_____

Statistician

_____

_____

The L2-quadrant (lower left)

Key words

The thinking preferences of the L2-quadrant include the following:

- **prefers traditional thinking (the way I know how)**
- **likes facts to be organised and orderly**
- **likes to work with detail**
- **prefers a stable and reliable environment**

- feels comfortable with procedure
- prefers security and safety to risk-taking
- facts must be sequential and chronological
- the task at hand is important – will complete it on time
- likes practical aspects

The person with strong L2 preferences would, therefore, prefer to organise and keep track of essential information. Projects are implemented on time, this person keeps a firm hand on financial matters and security is a priority. Once again, although your dominance in one or two of these categories may make you an L2 person, you might not be comfortable with all of them.

Careers

The person with strong L2 preferences would probably be involved in one of the following careers:

manager (particular environments)
storeman
supervisor
bookkeeper
legal profession
policeman
mapper
planner
secretary
organiser
administrator
militarist
school principal
typist

There are obviously other careers which fall in this category, but most important to this category is the preference of completing one task at a time and working according to a plan. The L2 person likes to structure and organise and to work in an orderly manner. He likes to feel safe within the work/home environment.

It is important to note, however, that some careers, depending on the type of duties in a specific company or department, may fall in more than one, or often all the quadrants. A secretary, for instance, will traditionally fall in the L2 and R2-quadrants (administrative, organised and people-orientated), but this may not always be the case – it depends on the company.

Going about your daily business
Buying a house

When buying a house, the person with strong L2 preferences would probably go about it (act and think) in the following way:

- *interested in safety and security*
- *interested in practical aspects such as size, space, storage, etc.*
- *the house should not be too 'different'*
- *must be comfortable*
- *location is important with regard to practical issues (schools, shops, doctor)*

Are you starting to understand the L2 (lower left) quadrant of the brain?

Activity

Do you think applicants applying for the following positions should have strong L2 preferences? Give reasons for your answers.

Building surveyor

Teacher

_____

_____

Magistrate

_____

_____

The R2-quadrant (lower right)

Key words

The person with a high score in the R2-quadrant, would prefer the following thinking processes:

- **facts experienced in an emotional way**
- **sympathetic and intuitive towards people**
- **likes interaction**
- **makes use of figurative language as well as non-verbal communication (body language, facial expressions, etc.)**
- **feels empathy towards others**
- **problem solving is often an emotional, not a logical process**
- **shows enthusiasm when he/she likes a new idea**

The person with strong R2 preferences would therefore have a 'feel' for people and situations, be able to read the body language of others and enjoy social interaction (one on one or within a group).

Careers

Careers suited to the person with strong R2 preferences include:

therapist
travel and tourism
market researcher
marketing (also in other quadrants)
selling
occupational therapist
journalist
negotiator
teacher
trainer (also in other quadrants)
minister of religion
nurse
social worker
waiter
TV and radio-related occupations

It goes without saying that there are more careers which will fall in this category, but the distinguishing characteristics are that people with these preferences seek interaction, involvement (physical and emotional) and need to "feel good" about their work situation and environment. It is important to note though, that some of the careers mentioned can also be placed in the other quadrants, depending on the specific duties and emphasis within a company. For example, someone involved in the selling of very advanced and technical commodities could also have strong L1 preferences.

Going about your daily business
Buying a house

The person with strong R2 preferences who is interested in buying a house would probably go about it in the following way:

- *needs to feel the comfort of the house – user-friendly*
- *needs to like it*
- *prefers a friendly house*

- *"feels" it is the right choice*
- *would like friends to recommend and support the choice*
- *regards entertainment possibilities as important*
- *does not want it to be too isolated*

Do you think you are starting to understand the R2 (lower right)-quadrant of the brain?

What R2 preferences would the following applicants have in common?

Nurse, social worker and psychologist?

_____

_____

Bank teller, financial adviser and teacher?

_____

_____

The R1-quadrant (top right)

Key words

The thinking processes preferred by a person with strong preferences in the R1-quadrant include the following:

- **seeing the whole picture, not detail**
- **likes change and trying new things**
- **enjoys being busy with several things at the same time**
- **has imagination**
- **does not readily accept "the only right answer", but looks for alternatives**
- **enjoys a challenge and a risk**

- can have a gut-feeling for new ideas
- can rearrange ideas and put them together into a new whole (synthesising)
- does not always do things in the same way
- likes to find a connection between the present and the future

The person with strong R1 preferences would therefore see the big picture rather than detail, recognise hidden possibilities, not always play according to the rules and act upon a gut-feeling rather than logic for problem solving; this person wants to do his or her 'own thing'.

Careers

The following are some of the careers which would be most suitable for people with strong R1 preferences:

skills trainer
leadership trainer
entrepreneur
advertiser
interior decorator
psychologist
paediatrician
architect
playwright
career in global tourism
career in training and development
civil/industrial engineer
strategist
futurist
landscape designer

Although these are traditionally R1 careers, some could also fall within the other quadrants, depending on the job description or the mission of the company. A paediatrician, for example, would also need to have strong R2 preferences (empathy, intuition).

Going about your daily business
Buying a house
   When buying a house, the person with strong R1 preferences would probably have the following approach:

- *notice the aesthetic qualities*
- *look for uniqueness*
- *must fit personal image, dreams*
- *must fit in with long-range plans*
- *wants to do things differently*
- *not really interested in detail*
- *will sometimes exceed his/her budget*
- *will take a risk*

Do you feel you understand the R1 (upper right)-quadrant of the brain better now?

When applying for the following positions, would applicants need a high, average or low score in the R1-quadrant? Give reasons for your answers.

Occupational therapist

_____

_____

Textile designer

_____

_____

Secretary

Combining preferences

It is important to note that many people have more than one dominant quadrant, or one dominant quadrant which is strongly supported by one or more of the other quadrants. This is very important when analysing a person's brain profile.

For example: a person with strong L1 (upper left) preferences and an interest in finance might choose to become an accountant or an actuary. This would be a good choice, unless the person has strong R2 preferences as well, which would mean he/she is people-orientated and enjoys interaction. A career as a financial adviser or a broker in which there is contact with people, would then be a more appropriate choice.

The values
The score values of The Neethling Brain Instrument are as follows:

95+	= very strong preference
80+	= strong preference
74 – 79	= strong average preference
65 – 73	= average preference
50 – 64	= low preference
50 and under	= very low preference/rejection

Your dominant quadrant is the quadrant in which you have the highest score.

Your secondary quadrant is the quadrant for which you show preference, but it is secondary to the primary quadrant.

Your tertiary quadrant is the quadrant with the lowest score and indicates low (or complete lack of) preferences.

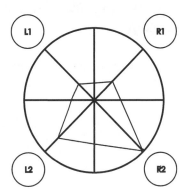

Dominant quadrant: R2
Secondary quadrant: L2
Tertiary quadrants: R1 and L1

In order to understand your thinking preferences better, study the following brain profiles and try to answer the questions on each profile. The dominant role played by thinking processes in choosing careers and selecting the right options will become clear to you. You may feel stupid for the simple reason that you have never pursued careers or options which are in line with your dominant thinking preferences.

Example 1

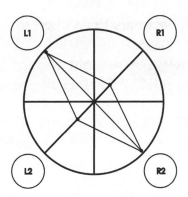

Name: Peter
Age: 17
Standard/Grade: Standard 10/Grade 12
School subjects: English C; Afrikaans C; Maths E; Accounting B; Economics B; Biology E

Which career choices would you suggest to Peter?

_____

_____

_____

Example 2

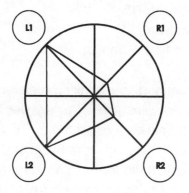

Name: Madelein
Age: 24
Highest qualification: Std 10/Grade 12
Present position: Secretary to an attorney

Is Madelein in the right position according to her brain profile? What other choices are open to her?

_____

_____

_____

Example 3

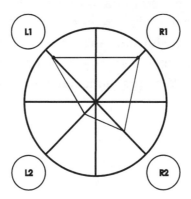

Name: Sharon
Age: 33
Highest qualification: Master's degree in Art
Present position: Art teacher at elementary/primary school

Why is Sharon frustrated with her job? What do you suggest could be done so that she can experience future fulfilment?

_____

_____

_____

Example 4

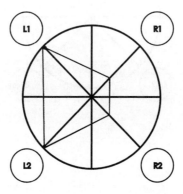

Name: Annette
Age: 35
Other information: Mother and part-time worker

Annette's son is a very creative child with strong right brain preferences. She is having difficulties dealing with him and keeping him occupied and happy. He is 5 years old. What are the reasons for this problem? What suggestions can you make for solving it?

_____

_____

_____

_____

Do you understand the brain profiles and can you apply your knowledge?

Plot the ideal brain profile of the following persons:

(a) A detective

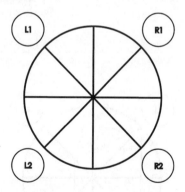

Explanation:

_____

_____

_____

(b) A minister of religion

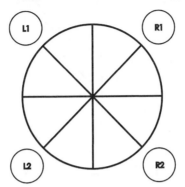

Explanation:

_____

_____

_____

(c) A fireman

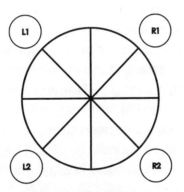

Explanation:

_____

_____

_____

(d) A ballet dancer

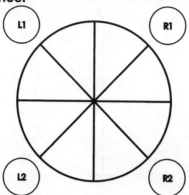

Explanation:

_____

_____

_____

What have you learned today?

Leo Buscaglia, who achieved well-deserved prominence with his books and articles on human relations, once said that his father had asked him every night what he had learned that specific day. He had to give an answer and this ritual which took place without fail night after night, made him a learner for life.

Before we move onto the next chapter you must try to remember the information you have been given on whole brain thinking. It could be beneficial to your sense of well-being, and generate passion and energy which could change your life forever.

Remember to expect miracles – because you are one.
– Anthony Robbins –

Creating

new

empowering

alternatives

Chapter 6

It should be clear to you by now that your brain profile is neither good nor bad, right nor wrong. Equipped with the knowledge of your own preferences, and also those of others, you will find that educational institutions, the home and the workplace can become 'happy' places – places where people do what they enjoy most, where they are encouraged to accept and understand differences and where opportunities exist for everyone to reach his/her full potential.

Once again Paul Torrance's words ring true: "Do the things you love doing and can do well." We all have the ability to do certain things well (our clever areas) and once we know what our thinking preferences are and we can combine our *clever* and our *preferences*, we become what we're supposed to be.

In Chapter 5 you were given the key words and basic information on the four quadrants of the brain. You discovered which preferences are associated with each of these quadrants.

You can of course have your brain profile plotted and analysed by professionals who have undergone training in this field. If you have not had this done, you will, however, have no difficulty in doing the following exercises, as you will have good insight into your preferences after reading Chapter 5.

Your own brain profile

Plot your brain profile

This activity is merely an indication of how the Neethling Brain Profile operates. A complete profile can be drawn up only if the official instrument is used.

Now plot your own brain profile (if you have not had it professionally done in which case you can write down the results you received). If you are going to plot the profile according to your own analysis you need to study the information in Chapter 5 first.

Follow these steps:
Step 1
From the qualities listed in the four blocks below, choose the three you prefer from each block. Write your twelve choices in the space provided (page 103).

Do not look at the score values before completing this exercise, as that may influence the result.

Block 1: Choose 3

planned
disciplined
methodical
organised
efficient
persistent
punctual
controlled

Am I clever or am I stupid?

Block 2: Choose 3

sensitive
intuitive
tolerant
receptive
eloquent
gentle
co-operative
trustworthy

Block 3: Choose 3

imaginative
searching
holistic
versatile
strategic
synthesising
adaptable
innovative

Block 4: Choose 3

factual
decisive
analytical
accurate
exploiting
rational
realistic
exact

Your twelve choices are:

1. _____
2. _____
3. _____
4. _____
5. _____
6. _____
7. _____
8. _____
9. _____
10. _____
11. _____
12. _____

Step 2

From the twelve choices above, now choose the five which describe you best and write them down in order of preference:

1. _____
2. _____
3. _____
4. _____
5. _____

Step 3

How to score

Choice 1 = 5 points

Choice 2 = 4 points

Choice 3 = 3 points

Choice 4 = 2 points

Choice 5 = 1 point

The blocks on the previous pages represent the four quadrants:

Am I clever **or am I** stupid?

Block 1 = L2
Block 2 = R2
Block 3 = R1
Block 4 = L1

Use the information *How to score* given above to fill in the following:

Choice	Block	Quadrant	Points
e.g. 1st	1	L2	5
1st			
2nd			
3rd			
4th			
5th			

Totals:

L1 = _____
L2 = _____
R2 = _____
R1 = _____

Step 4

Now plot your profile using the following circle: (If you score 0 in any quadrant, give yourself a score of 1)

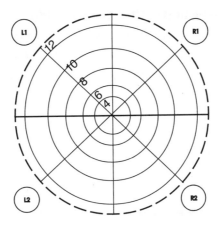

Plotting your brain profile in this way might not give you a perfectly accurate profile, but it is a good indication of the thinking processes you prefer.

Can you answer the following questions regarding your brain profile?

● Which quadrant is your dominant quadrant?

_____

● Which quadrant(s) is/are your secondary quadrant(s)?

_____

● Which quadrant(s) is/are your tertiary quadrant(s)?

_____

Activity

Analysing your brain profile

Analyse your own brain profile using the tables below. It is important to be honest with yourself. Refer to Chapter 5 if you need to refresh your memory or you need more information. Take time to reflect on the things you enjoy most, how you usually tackle problems, how you react in unusual or new situations. When you look at the key words for

each quadrant as listed in Chapter 5, decide in which quadrant you find most of your preferences, the fewest preferences or where you consider your preferences to be average, etc. Now you should be ready to analyse your own brain profile.

Table 1

According to your brain profile, indicate your:

Dominant preferences	Secondary preferences	Tertiary preferences

Have you learnt anything new about yourself, or has something which has puzzled you about yourself at times, suddenly become clear?

_____

_____

_____

Table 2

Fill in the following information regarding your chosen career (present, or past if you are not working at the moment, or your prospective career if you are a student):

Your chosen career	Preferences required for this career	Your preferences according to your profile

After completing the table above, answer the following questions regarding your career choice:

● Have you chosen the right career?

_____

● Why?

_____

● According to your profile, what other career options are open to you?

_____

_____

● Answer True or False to the following statements regarding your brain preferences:

- I prefer completing one task at a time, rather than being busy with many tasks at the same time.

- I prefer security to taking risks.

- I can sense people's problems in an intuitive way.

- I prefer information to be given in an orderly and chronological manner.

The following derogatory phrases are often used by people to describe those with brain preferences which differ from their own. In which quadrants would your place people who fit the following descriptions?

"blowing hot and cold"
"conservative stick-in-the-mud"
"a cold fish"
"way out"
"easy meat"
"can lead him by the nose"
"pedantic"
"always nit-picking"
"nerd"
"insensitive"
"painfully tidy"

L1-quadrant

_____

_____

L2-quadrant

_____

_____

R2-quadrant

_____

_____

R1-quadrant

_____

_____

 Test your insights

Advertisements

Studying the brain preferences of people around you can be fun and it can become an interesting pastime! Certain brain preferences are revealed not only by people we know, but also by characters in movies or books. A home reveals the preferences of the person(s) who decorated it and different advertisements usually target specific quadrant groups.

Do the following two advertisements reveal certain information which you might not have noticed before? Study them and then answer the questions in the spaces provided below them.

(1) Which quadrant group (or groups) would be most impressed by this advertisement? Why?

(2) Which quadrant group (or groups) would be least impressed or affected by this advertisement? Why?

(3) Judging by your answers in (1) and (2), do you think the advertisers selected the correct advertising style for this particular product?

(4) Does this advertisement impress *you*? Why? Why not?

(5) What is being advertised? (Not the product, but the concept, eg love, safety, etc.)

Advertisement 1

(1) _____

_____

(2) _____

_____

(3) _____

_____

(4) _____

_____

(5) _____

_____

Advertisement 2

(1) _____

_____

(2) _____

_____

(3) _____

_____

(4) _____

_____

(5) _____

_____

Articles

Have you ever read an article which you enjoyed, or hated, because of the way it was written? The reason could be found in both the reporter's and your brain profiles – they were either similar or direct opposites. The following three reports on the same topic illustrate the different views of the reporters who wrote them. Which is the dominant quadrant of each of these reporters?

Article 1

I am talking to Dr Charles in his spacious house with its broad passages and white walls, in the North West Province mining town of Klerksdorp (South Africa). All the equipment is ready in the room where he will perform his abortions. He explains the procedure: the woman will be examined and given an injection to relax her muscles. Then a local anaesthetic is administered to the uterus and the fetus is removed by suction. The procedure takes 10 to 15 minutes. After an hour's rest, the woman can go home. According to Dr Charles there is no risk to the patient.

Quadrant: _____

Article 2

I feel my throat tightening as Dr Charles leads me into the clinically clean and white rooms where, he tells me, he will soon put an end to unwanted pregnancies. As he explains the procedure, it is what goes unsaid that is shouted from the walls: the terrified faces, the suffering, the lives lost. When I manage to escape and smell the flowers in the garden again I know that the first seed of doubt about the new-found freedom in the New South Africa has been planted in my soul.

Quadrant: _____

Article 3

Narrative

Self-proclaimed Klerksdorp abortionist, Dr Charles, is lobbying for the legalisation of abortions in South Africa. A recent poll found that 6 per cent of the 1 500 doctors questioned were in favour of more lenient abortion laws, but the Pro Life organisation insists that each human being has the right to life. What is happening in other countries? In most European countries and some states in America abortion has been legalised. I agree a decision here in South Africa has to be made, but not without the realisation that we have a responsibility to future generations. What will our decision say about our moral state, our humanity and our values? We certainly have to be open to change and to the risk of change – but with our finger on the pulse of tomorrow.

Quadrant: _____

Journeying within and without

Now that you have gained new insight into your thinking preferences and established your present brain profile, it is time to take action. As someone once said: To desire is to obtain; to aspire is to achieve. This *aspire* means to use your insights and your *clever* abilities.

The oak sleeps in the acorn; the bird waits in the egg; and in the highest vision of the soul a walking angel stirs. Dreams are the seedlings of realities.
– James Allen –

Applying the whole brain

Chapter 7

It is important to understand that on our journey of rediscovery, the focus is not on where we come from, but who we are now. You are now able to understand and utilise clever abilities you might never have thought possible. Decide now what you want to become; carry on making this decision consciously, passionately and energetically. And then do something about it.

Historical and cultural factors are often stumbling-blocks and obstruct the implementation of whole brain thinking. A school, organisation or company that was highly successful once, but has fallen into a rut over the years, is not open to change. Even when it becomes quite clear that change is inevitable, those within the situation rarely notice this until, in most cases, it is already too late.

A more important factor which possibly prevents whole brain management, leadership, negotiation, and the whole brain approach to any other sphere of life, is the ignorance which exists about its nature and impact. For example, very often people are inclined to confuse right brain activity with artistic talent.

When the preferences of employees have been determined, management will be in a position to effectively and skillfully direct, place and utilise employees according to their individual preferences. This will have an immediate effect on production and service as well as on an interpersonal level.

 Applying the whole brain: in management

Job applications

If you wish, you can take another look at the examples given in Chapter 5.

Brain profiling has become an essential part of selecting the most suitable candidate for the job. It is important to remember however, that brain preferences and skills do not automatically go together. A profile may therefore reveal a strong preference for strategic and conceptual thinking without the person having received any training in this field.

On the other hand, a person may be a very competent and well-qualified accountant, yet he dislikes his work. Thus he lacks the enthusiasm and energy necessary to sustain him in his vision.

Lack of preference does not limit competency, but it will not generate the same passion and motivation for one's work.

Appointing someone in a position which is not in alignment with his/her preferences could therefore mean that this person

- will constantly be on the look-out for something else;
- becomes frustrated and disillusioned;
- will avoid or lose interest in his colleagues because they think "differently";
- will hamper growth and development because of an inability to realise his or her own dreams.

Very often frustration within a company can be solved by determining the preferences of employees and then moving them to other departments or changing their duties to suit their preferences.

Let's see whether you can implement brain profiling if you have to decide on the best person for the job.

Activity

Write a job description, as you see it, for the entertainment manager of a large hotel.

_____

_____

_____

_____

_____

_____

Now plot his/her brain profile

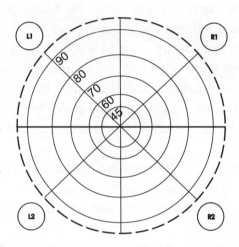

Problem solving

Very often problems within a company or department or in the home are not solved, because of conflicting ideas. Once a manager/parent/leader realises that these opposing ideas are the result of a difference in thinking preferences of the people concerned, these very differences can be used in a positive way.

The essence is, of course, to cultivate a whole brain culture within a company or home and to ensure that all employees/family members have at least a basic knowledge of the meaning of whole brain management. We think, work, live, play in different ways – this should be acknowledged by everyone. These differences should not be seen in a negative light, but as an asset in the problem solving process.

The person who solves problems in a logical way should have understanding for the person who solves problems by 'a feel for' the facts. Keeping an open mind about differences can help to solve problems, whereas a resistance to different views can thwart a positive outcome.

Study the following whole brain problem solving table:

L1
- analyses the facts
- wants things to be correct
- sees the facts clearly – devoid of emotion
- gathers all information
- has a neutral stance (is objective)
- sees problems rationally
- deals with facts in a logical way
- focuses on preciseness/exactness

L 2
- organises/arranges the facts (in categories and/or according to a plan)
- deals with the facts chronologically
- checks the facts
- can be critical of ideas
- finds faults and weaknesses in ideas of others (challenging) can see danger of new solutions
- seeks detail and elaboration of these
- practical aspects important
- prefers tried and tested methods

R 1
- solves problems in an intuitive way
- sees the big picture
- visualises the facts (also big picture vision)
- is full of ideas and stimulating
- sees opportunity and likes to speculate

- likes alternatives
- often has new and innovative ideas
- likes to take risks

R 2
- suggestions often emotional
- has an intuitive feel for people involved
- values are important
- feelings of suspicion and jealousy might limit vision
- usually eager to share ideas
- often brings new insight to the idea
- enthusiastic about ideas
- human aspects are fundamental

Whole brain problem solving can bring about unique solutions which would be impossible if only one or two quadrants are utilised in the problem solving process. The interaction of different thinking processes not only creates creative breakthrough, but it also establishes the necessary control and balance. For example, the L2 thinker might recognise a potential threat posed by a proposed solution, something which nobody else would have thought of. The R2 thinker can sometimes – simply because of a gut feeling and a seemingly illogical process, come up with possibilities which would never have crossed anybody's mind.

Decision making
The problem solving table can also be used as a guide to whole brain decision making.

Do you understand your own style of problem solving and decision making any better now?

Activity

Write down 5 major decisions you have made recently and then draw the brain profile of each of these decisions.

Example: I am going to keep all my financial records straight and up to date and cut down on impulsive buying.

(1) _____

_____

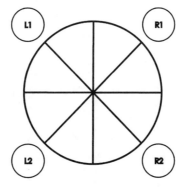

(2) _____

_____

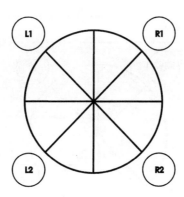

Am I clever or am I stupid?

(3)_____

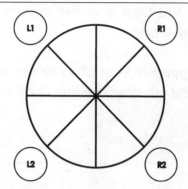

(4)_____

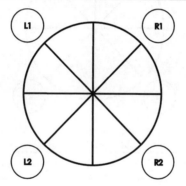

(5)_____

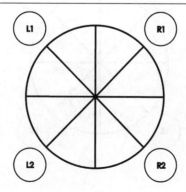

What does your profile have to do with decision making?

To be a top decision maker, you should have certain characteristics. Add four to the list below:

- **be prepared to take risks**
- **be innovative/creative**
- **tolerate ambiguity**
- **be a good listener**

- _____
- _____
- _____
- _____

Applying the whole brain: in teaching (training)

The learning place most probably has the greatest need of a whole brain culture. Profiling the brain preferences of the child and student in the early stages would certainly result in better subject and career choices.

Teachers/instructors ought to be conscious of the fact that a class does not consist of one group of like-minded thinkers, but of a variety of different thinkers. Each student has his/her own preferences and will thus enjoy his studies, the teaching he is subjected to, the atmosphere in the class and the type of projects he has to complete only if these are compatible with his brain preferences.

The teacher/instructor will, of course, teach mainly according to his/her own preferences. Furthermore, the school system has always been traditionally left brain orientated, with the result that right brain thinkers in the teaching profession have adopted left brain teaching styles in order to 'fit in'. Normally the student with left brain preferences is suitably catered for in the classroom, but there are a vast number of learners who never reach their full potential, who never experience any pleasure in learning, because their brain preferences are simply not in line with those of the teacher or the system.

The whole brain classroom

When preparing a classroom the teacher/instructor will have to take into account the thinking preferences of the various students. It stands to reason that parents should take these facts into account when deciding on the correct study environment for their children. To accommodate all (or at least most of the thinking preferences), a classroom should have the following features:

L1
- tidy
- information readily available
- information on numbers, mass/weights, etc. on display
- very accurate blackboard/chalkboard work

L2
- organised content
- programmes, lists, time-tables at hand
- detailed blackboard/chalkboard work, well-organised

R1
- visual displays
- colour
- creative and evocative information
- humorous displays

- artistic content
- metaphors

R2
- space for movement
- music in background (at intervals)
- colour
- people-orientated visual displays
- comfortable

Whole brain teaching/training

Important information

Once a teacher/trainer has accepted that a class consists of pupils/students with distinctive brain preferences, she can vary her teaching methods and so accommodate the different kinds of thinkers.

L1 teaching/training
During L1 teaching the lesson will include the following:

- formal lesson
- use of a text book
- the use of summaries
- logical arguments
- clear articulation
- precise instructions
- opportunity to analyse content
- opportunity for research
- opportunity to discuss technical aspects

L2 teaching/training
The L2 lesson will consist of the following:

- the use of a text book

- content presented in sequential order
- well-planned lesson content
- clearly structured lesson
- opportunity to put content into practice
- clear instructions – repeated to reinforce
- lesson objectives must be clear
- formal lesson

R2 teaching/training
The R2 lesson will include the following:

- opportunity for interaction with others (group work)
- opportunity for movement
- music on a regular basis
- opportunity to relate lesson content with personal experience (or with that of others)
- opportunity to show emotions regarding lesson content
- opportunity to be teacher/trainer

R1 teaching/training
- give holistic view of lesson
- allow spontaneous participation
- visual aids, etc
- opportunity to relate content to past or future
- aesthetics
- opportunity to experiment
- introduce new concepts
- emphasis on uniqueness (doing own thing)
- opportunities for fun things (even the absurd!)

Whole brain learning
If one takes into account the information on whole brain teaching, it becomes quite clear that there are differences – not only in the way a student prefers to be taught, but also the way in which a student prefers to study.

Study the following whole brain learning table. Now draw a profile of your (or/and your children's) preferences.

L1 learning
- makes use of summaries
- studies alone
- makes use of a text book
- analyses the content
- neat desk
- studies according to precise instructions
- focus on memory and information

L2 learning
- uses summaries
- studies according to a timetable/programme
- organised desk
- keeps at it till he/she has acquired the knowledge
- studies in a secure and organised environment

R2 learning
- music
- shares ideas while studying
- studies in a group (or with one or two other people)
- talks out loud
- moves around while studying
- dramatising of content

R1 learning
- pleasant surroundings
- surroundings not necessarily tidy
- studies with visual aids
- synthesises content
- likes to add action to content
- likes to experiment

Your learning profile:

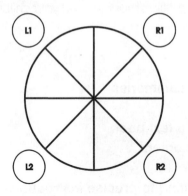

The whole brain question paper

If we acknowledge that there are students with different brain preferences in one class, it follows that the classroom and teaching style should be adapted to suit all students for at least part of the teaching process. It also stands to reason that projects and question papers should be set in such a way that all the preference groups are accommodated.

Narrative

Look at the following example of a comprehension test:

One day I will start a chewing gum factory

I will sell 'thinking gum' especially designed for the exams, and maybe 'erase-a-freckle gum' for some of my girlfriends. Mrs Smith would appreciate a 'headache gum' and for Mr Frost 'stop-smoking gum' would be just the thing. Naturally my 'lose-weight gum' will be a hit – especially if I make it look like a measuring tape.

Let me think ... maybe 'grow-some-hair gum' or 'no-more-toothpaste gum' could also work.

Of course, 20% of chewing gum consists of wheat. An ear of wheat consists of bran, starch, gluten and wheat germ. The gluten is the magic power, the starch is there for energy, the bran forms the outside layer and the germ contains the embryo of the new plant.

This has actually given me an idea. If wheat is supposed to be good for you, I need to use that fact in my advertising. Mmmm …'Chew and stay healthy'…

Questions

L1 question:
(1) Name the different types of chewing gum the author thought of. (factual)

L2 question:
(2) List the ingredients of an ear of corn and next to it write down the functions of each. (structured)

R2 question:
(3) Which of the gum mentioned would you like best and why? (feeling)

R1 question:
(4) Invent your own new gum and write an advertisement for it. (innovative)

How about you? With the knowledge of whole brain teaching you have acquired, can you set a whole brain question paper?

Activity

Add one question of your own for each of the quadrants on the comprehension test above:

L1:_____

_____

L2:_____

_____

R2:_____

_____

R1:_____

_____

A Grade 7 class has to study a map of the world. Think of four different projects to give the class on this topic, choosing one for each quadrant.

L1:_____

_____

L2:_____

_____

R2:_____

_____

R1:_____

_____

Elevate your thoughts

It is universally accepted that the same kind of thinking which brought us where we are today will not take us where we want to be tomorrow. If you have decided to go the whole brain route, start *doing* what you *now know*. Keep on practising your whole brain insights.

For the next seven days (starting right now) commit yourself to the following course of action: the application of your whole brain knowledge in your different environments:

- at home (a different way of thinking about your family members)

Applying the whole brain

- at work (whole brain understanding of your colleagues)
- at school (whole brain teaching and learning)
- watching television (television advertisements: left/right brain)
- keep on refreshing your life.

Nothing splendid has ever been achieved except by those who dared believe that something inside of them was superior to their circumstances.

– Bruce Barton –

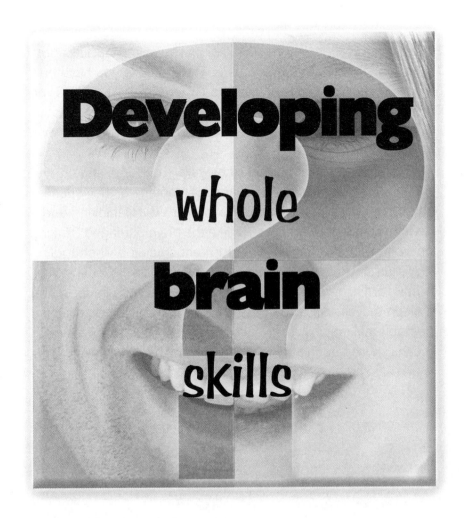

Developing whole brain skills

Chapter 8

So what we have been saying in this book all along, is that the way you think about yourself, about life, about anything, determines who you are. The thoughts you have built into your character have brought you where you are – and as you change your thoughts you change your life. You are a creative human being and thus the creator and manager of your own circumstances.

Research on exceptional achievers (both individuals and organisations) indicates that a large percentage of their success can be attributed to an openness in their way of thinking and a general sense of awareness. Unlike the brain-damaged thinking one often finds in disfunctional bureaucracies and struggling individuals, whole brain empowerment combats closed thinking. Whole brain empowerment of successful organisations and their employees will also acknowledge the thinking potential and decision-making abilities of each individual. Thus cleverness also means staying open and gaining access to healthy thinking. This is an ongoing process of renewal.

 Brainstorming – revisiting an old concept

Nothing is more dangerous than an idea when it's the only one you have.
– Emile Chartier –

When we discussed the primary skills of the creative thinker in Chapter 2, the importance of being a fluent thinker became very clear. If you want to come up with one good idea, it is important to first generate many ideas.

Unfortunately this is why many people never start the creative process – they do not know how to be idea generators. Like any other skill, this skill has to be practised. In this chapter you are going to be introduced to different skills and techniques of brainstorming which will incorporate the development of whole brain thinking skills.

One of the reasons why the creative idea (the 'aha') keeps on eluding us is that we are often blinded by the 'one right answer' and therefore reluctant to think of other possibilities. We want to get the problem out of the way as soon as possible and consequently go for the first possible answer or solution. The other side of the coin is that as soon as we we start looking for alternatives, for something else, we open up our imagination to let the creative ideas in.

 Osborn (*Applied Imagination*, 1963) laid down four rules for brainstorming which provide important guidelines. They are:

- **No negative criticism; delay judgment until a considerable number of alternatives have been generated.**
- **Freewheeling is recommended; the wilder the ideas the better.**
- **Quantity is important; include the small, obvious alternatives as well as the wilder, more unusual, clever ones.**
- **Combine alternatives and hitch a ride on these alternatives to produce new ones.**

The concept brainstorming has unfortunately been misused in workshops, seminars, decision-making groups – just about everywhere. Simply getting together in groups to discuss problems is often automatically called brainstorming. Osborne meant brainstorming to be a creative process, not a rehash of old familiar ideas and arguments. (See: *Applied Imagination*.)

Today brainstorming is often alternated with processes generally called:

- left or right brain idea generation
- whole brain idea generation
- feeling/emotion generation
- creativity processing

For successful brainstorming, a psychological openness is required – a postponement of judgment. If this does not happen, the creative process is severely inhibited.

The rules for brainstorming do not, however, apply to the idea-seeking stage only. When an idea has been selected and the planning of its implementation starts, it is once again important to brainstorm the different ways in which the new idea can be implemented, its possible consequences, etc.

The process of problem *finding* is probably the most neglected step in an attempt at finding alternatives.

Individuals and organisations almost always take it for granted that the problem has already been identified. The assumption exists that the nature of the problem is obvious and all that is necessary is for it to be solved. The breakthrough to new markets, new products and services as well as creative solutions to political, economic, educational and virtually every other problem is frustrated because the initial definition of the problem is addressed instead of its *essence*.

Such a wrong (or partly wrong) approach to problem solving can lead to:

- delayed solution finding
- apparent initial success, but later on it becomes quite clear that the real problem has not been addressed

- a waste of money
- a waste of time
- wasteful and ineffective use of manpower
- a process which will ultimately lead to frustration, deterioration and decline.

Development of left brain skills

The following are techniques for developing the creative skills of the left hemisphere of the brain.

The L1-quadrant: Method 635

This technique is normally used for groups of six people, but can be adapted for smaller groups as well. The steps involve the following:

- **Identify the problem you want to solve or the situation you would like to improve.**
- **Allow five minutes in which each of the 6 persons in the group writes down 3 ideas on idea cards (postcard size).**
- **Each card is then passed on to the next person who develops the idea by adding attributes. This is done five times.**
- **After 30 minutes about 108 ideas should have been developed.**
- **The group is now given the opportunity to discuss the ideas on the table. The participants are encouraged to evaluate each idea.**
- **The group then makes a selection of the best ideas.**

The L1-quadrant: attribute splitting

The idea behind the attribute splitting technique is to split the components of a problem into different parts and then to put them together again in a variety of ways.

These are the steps to follow:

1. State your problem (challenge) in two words, capturing the essence. For example, if your challenge is, "In which ways can I manage my time better", the two words could be 'time management'.

2. Place these two attributes into two separate blocks of a diagram (see the example below).

3. Split each of these two attributes into two more attributes. There is, of course, no right or wrong way of splitting the original attributes – it will depend on your perspective of the problem.

4. Repeat the activity of splitting the attributes until you feel satisfied that you have enough material to work with.

5. Study each attribute with an open mind. Try to find hidden ideas in them.

6. Combine the attributes. Try as many alternatives as possible.

Example

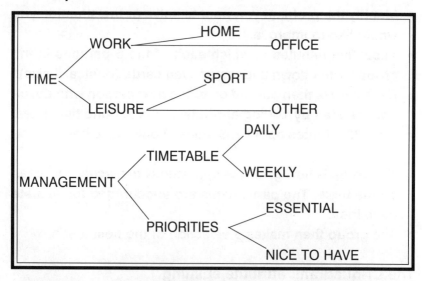

Now you could select one of the attributes to focus on, e.g. 'nice to have' and list all the things you enjoy doing and having, but which could be cut out of your daily activities. Or you could link 'sport', 'weekly' and 'timetable' and work out a weekly timetable for your sports activities. This could cut down on travelling or other time-consuming aspects.

The L2-quadrant: Scamper

The word *Scamper* is derived from the first letters of the seven key words of the process:

Substitute
Combine
Adapt
Magnify, minimise, multiply
Put to other uses
Else
Rearrange

Follow the steps of the *scamper* technique in a systematic and structured way.

Let's see if you can scamper!

 You work for a company that supplies soft drinks to shops. As a sideline, you also supply them with ice. You feel this part of the service is not fully utilised. Use the scamper technique to try and solve this problem.

- **S = Substitute**
  With what can you *substitute* it?

  - **Who else?**
  - **What else?**
  - **Other ingredient?**
  - **Other material?**
  - **Other process?**
  - **Other power?**

- **Other place?**
- **Other approach?**

- **C = Combine**
  What can you *combine*?

  - **What about a blend, a partnership, an amalgamation?**
  - **Combine units?**
  - **Combine objectives?**
  - **Combine ideas?**

- **A = Adapt**
  What can you *adapt*?

  - **What else is exactly like this?**
  - **What other idea does this suggest?**
  - **What can I copy?**
  - **Who can I emulate?**

_____

_____

_____

_____

_____

_____

- **M = Magnify, minimise, multiply**
  Can you *magnify, minimise, multiply*?

  - **What to add?**
  - **More time?**
  - **Stronger, higher, longer?**
  - **Enlarge?**
  - **What to deduct?**
  - **Smaller?**
  - **Condensed?**
  - **Omit?**
  - **Split up?**
  - **More of?**

_____

_____

_____

_____

_____

_____

- **P = Put to other uses**
  Can you use it for something else?

  - **New ways to use it as it is?**

- **Other uses if modified?**

_____

_____

_____

_____

_____

_____

- **E = Else**
  Alternatives

  - **What else?**
  - **Who else?**
  - **Where else?**
  - **How else?**

_____

_____

_____

_____

_____

- **R = Rearrange, reverse**
  Can you rearrange?

  - **Interchange components?**
  - **Other pattern?**
  - **Change pace?**
  - **Change schedule?**
  - **Turn the other cheek?**
  - **Reverse roles?**

- **Transpose positive and negative?**

_____

_____

_____

_____

_____

_____

The L2-quadrant: Checklist Technique

1. Write down your problem (challenge). Also write down "re-solved by date" and commit yourself to solving the problem by this date.

2. Ask as many questions as possible by using the checklist below.

3. Keep records, lists, tables and diagrams of all the answers in order to evaluate and analyse them later.

The checklist technique: questions

The problem

- What is the essence of the problem?
- What do you need in order to solve the problem?
- What information, etc. do you have on the problem?
- Is there any information you can discard?
- What is not part of the problem?
- What about the problem do you not understand?
- Can you split the problem into attributes? What are they?
- Are any of these attributes fixed (unchangeable)?
- Is this a new problem for you?
- Is any part of the problem familiar to you?
- Are you aware of a problem related to this one?
- If yes, what are the similarities between the problems?

- Was this related problem solved?
- Can you use the same solution?
- What can you gain by solving the problem?
- What is the worst that can happen if you do not find a solution?
- Are you following your own or somebody else's rules in the solution finding process?
- Can the rules be changed?
- Can you rephrase your problem in as many different ways as possible?

The plan

- Can you visualise a solution?
- How many of the unknown aspects of the problem can you determine by using your information?
- What else can you derive from your information?
- Do you need more information?
- Have you written down all the aspects and issues involved?
- Have you decided on steps to follow in the problem solving process?
- Have you used alternatives in finding the solution?
- Have you considered how others have solved a similar problem?
- How many and which thinking techniques can you use in order to find a creative solution?
- How many different solutions are possible?
- Which changes will these bring about? What do you need to do now/later?
- What must others to do? What and who?
- How should you/others do it?
- Can you add other problems to this one in order to solve them simultaneously?
- In which way(s) is this problem unique?
- Which results will be an indication of success?
- How can you be sure that you are making progress?

- How can you determine whether you will find a solution within your time limit?

Development of right brain skills

The following are brainstorming techniques for developing the creative skills of the right hemisphere of the brain.

The R2-quadrant: Sociodrama

(For further information consult Paul Torrance's latest publication, *Creative Role Playing* (1996), which is probably the most major contribution to sociodrama ever published.)

The majority of creativity techniques involve, to some extent, R2 processing. Whenever the individual interacts with other members in the group, the R2 comes into play.

A group (teachers, physicians, supervisors, etc.) can use sociodrama to learn and practise better ways of dealing with certain kinds of people, and to understand the inherent conflict in particular relationships.

Sociodrama can be used as a tool for problem solving from the classroom to the boardroom. It can be applied:

- **to develop social roles**
- **for practising decision making**
- **to facilitate interpersonal relationships**
- **to develop new insights and breakthroughs**

The objective of sociodrama is to examine a group or a social problem by making use of drama.

Sociodrama as a creative problem-solving process usually follows these steps:

Am I clever or am I stupid?

❑ **Defining the problem**

The director, leader or teacher should explain to the group that they are going to participate in an unrehearsed skit and try to find ways of solving some problem which concerns all of them.

It is a good idea to begin by asking a series of questions to help define the problem and establish the conflict situation. At this point the leader takes note of all responses to get as many facts as possible, to increase understanding of the problem and to verbalise it more effectively. He asks other questions to stimulate or provoke further thoughts about the real problem or conflict. This produces what Parnes (1967) refers to as 'the fuzzy problem' or 'the mess' which makes it possible to determine or establish the conflict situation (stating the problem).

❑ **Determining a situation (conflict)**

By sifting the responses, the leader must now describe a conflict situation in objective and understandable terms. No indication is given as to the direction the solution should take. As in creative problem solving, judgment is withheld. The conflict situation runs parallel with problem definition in the creative problem solving model.

❑ **Casting of characters**

Participation should be voluntary. The leader however, should make a point of watching the audience for new roles which might emerge. He/she must also encourage the timid person who really wants to participate and is saying this by means of body language. Roles should rarely be allocated in advance. Several members of the group may play one particular role, each using a different approach.

❑ **Briefing and warming up actors and observers**

It is usually a good idea to give the actors a few minutes to plan the set and to come to an agreement on general matters. While the actors are out of the room, the leader prepares the observers

Developing whole brain skills

for possible alternatives. Members of the audience might be asked to identify with one or other of the main characters or to observe them from a particular viewpoint. When the actors return to the room, they can be asked to describe the scene and explain their role identities. This is a brief, but relaxed procedure, which puts both the audience and the actors at ease.

❏ **Acting out the situation**

Acting out the situation may take a few seconds, or it might last for 10 to 20 minutes. As a leader gains experience as a sociodrama director, she will be able to use a variety of production techniques to probe even deeper into the problem, to increase the number and originality of the alternatives, to get members out of their thinking ruts, and to get them to dare bigger mental leaps in the process of finding better solutions.

The leader should watch for areas of conflict among group members, but he should not give clues or hints concerning the desired outcome. If the acting breaks down because a participant has forgotten his lines, the leader may encourage the actor by saying, "What happens now?" If this does not work, it may be necessary or advisable to 'cut' the action.

❏ **Cutting the action**
The action should be stopped or cut whenever

- the actors' role-play is hopelessly wide of the mark, or they experience a serious block and are unable to continue;
- the episode comes to a conclusion;
- the leader sees an opportunity to stimulate thinking to a higher level of creativity by using a different episode.

❏ **Discussing and analysing the situation, the behaviour and the ideas produced.**
There are various approaches to a discussion and analysis of what takes place in a sociodrama. When a leader makes use of

the creative problem-solving model, he or she would most probably formulate certain directives for discussing and evaluating contributions made by the actors and the audience. It should be a controlled type of discussion in any event, leaving room for guidance, with the leader assisting the group in redefining the problem and identifying various possible solutions indicated by the action.

❏ **Planning subsequent testing and/or the implementation of ideas for new behaviour**
There are a variety of practices around the planning of further testing and/or implementation of ideas generated for new and improved behaviour resulting from the sociodrama.

If there is time, or if there are to be subsequent sessions, the new ideas can be tested in a new sociodrama.

Or, plans might correlate with applications outside of the sociodrama sessions. This step runs parallel with the selling, planning and implementation stages in creative problem solving. The technique of role-playing in preparing people to sell and/or implement new solutions has been widely used for quite some time.

Activity

Would you be able to use the sociodrama technique of brainstorming?

Situation 1
Problems have arisen at a school because many pupils flatly disregard rules concerning the proper school uniform.

Situation 2
Problems have arisen at a factory because workers are unhappy about the allocation of flexi-hours and overtime.

How can sociodrama be applied to solve these problems and which roles would you make use of in each situation?

Situation 1:

_____

_____

_____

_____

_____

_____

Situation 2:

_____

_____

_____

_____

_____

The R2-quadrant: Sensory Awareness Model

We derive the knowledge and pleasure that each of us gets from our environment by means of two distinct learning processes: reasoning and sensory involvement. Unfortunately we rarely learn from our immediate perceptions. The following technique can open up your mind to fresh ideas, at the same time developing your sensory awareness.

Select any object found in nature (pine-cone, flower, etc.). This technique was originally created and compiled by Michael F. Andrews. Andrews suggests that you use an object which attracts you personally, or even something you have become obsessed with.

● **Study the object; not in the conventional way, but care-**

fully; see if you can detect some kind of awareness around the object.

- Fix your mind upon direct, immediate, personal and emotional responses.
- What does it *look* like? Note the shape, parts, colour, texture, design, etc. (visual sensation).
- What does it *sound* like? Listen intently, rub the object, move it around. Does the sound change? What do the sounds do to you?
- What does the object *feel* like? Note the sensation of touch. What do the various surfaces of the object feel like?
- What does the object *smell* like? Is it a fragrant scent, spicy, pleasant, repulsive? Think about the effect the smell has on you.
- What does the object *taste* like? Explore the wide range of tastes. Start over and relish the taste.
- Allow your different sensory experiences to intermingle. Example:
  - What does the *colour* of the pine-cone *taste* like?
  - What does the *fragrance* of the pine-cone *look* like?

Sensory awareness can be developed!

The R1-Quadrant: Semantic intuition

This technique is easy to use in the workplace (or at home) when problems arise.

Activity

Try to solve the problem given below by following the five steps of this technique.

Situation:
You are the manager of a shopping center. You have received complaints from customers that your center offers no entertainment for children.

Steps:

1. Define the problem:

What could we do to keep our customers who have children happy?

2. Identify two key elements of the problem. (See the example given in the table below.)

3. Generate ideas pertaining to each element.

Entertainment for customers	
Eg. mothers	children
	play groups

4. Combine ideas listed in one column with ideas from the next, e.g. *play group mothers*.

_____

_____

_____

_____

_____

_____

5. Use the combinations to form new ideas (solutions), e.g. use mothers on a rotation basis to take charge of a play group for say 30 minutes at a time.

_____

_____

_____

_____

_____

_____

The R1-quadrant: Word-association

 This technique reminds one of a game children like to play. Choose any word. Use a dictionary, a magazine or any other reading matter and choose a word at random. Then, at least five times, write down a word which you associate with the previous one. Look at the following example:

Fish

▼

Catch

▼

Thief

▼

Steal

▼

Heart

▼

Beat

Now relate each word-association that you made in this way to your problem. Say for example the problem you need to solve is, "How can we impove communication in our company (at home, etc.)?", then these words can help you as follows:

Thief: We need to establish what is disrupting our communication (robbing us of good communication) and then handle it as harshly as we would a thief.

Heart: We need to determine the people's needs regarding communication and try to come up to these expectations.

Now add two more words to the examples given above and then associate all the words that have not been used with the above-mentioned problem.

This technique teaches you to make connections between things and words which do not normally go together, but which often lead to amazing breakthroughs.

Development of whole brain skills: The synergy

Mind Mapping

 The whole brain technique 'mind mapping', is a way in which we can communicate with our own minds. Often the images in our minds are not clear and we find it difficult to hold on to thoughts. When however, you draw your thoughts, like you would a map, a communication process starts. This is mind mapping and by doing this you are not only able to record thoughts as they occur, but also change, manipulate and combine ideas as your mind map takes shape. Do not worry about neatness or try to be too organised when mapping; just as long as you understand what it all means. You can start by stating a problem you cannot solve and then add any thoughts, feelings and impressions which relate to it. Try to find ideas while studying the map. And please note, it takes concentration!

Each map is the unique creation of its owner. There are, however, a few basic steps to follow when mapping your thoughts.

Although the map displays thoughts as they occur, you must have some form of order in your map. You may use the cartoonist's thinking bubbles, connecting lines, colour to group information together, the same letter size for information of similar importance, etc. Although there are no set rules on arranging your information, you should have no problem understanding your own map if you make use of some of the following hints:

- **Don't write long sentences – simply jot down key words.**
- **When studying your map, combine words and phrases (even if they seem completely unrelated) in order to create new ideas.**

• When studying your map, think of a bunch of grapes and bunch all the thoughts together which could form a new whole. This will help you spot gaps which need to be filled with new information.

• When mind mapping, concentrate on your problem and the possible solutions your map can offer. This requires an increased mental awareness and involvement in the thinking processes which are taking place all the time. Become one with your map on a mental level, move thoughts around, combine, reposition, regroup, etc.

BE ALERT!

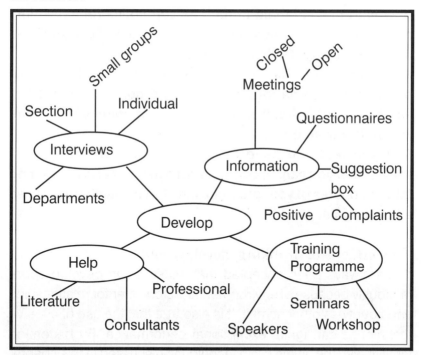

Whole brain: Symbol Technique

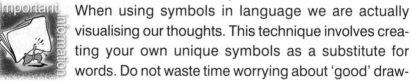 When using symbols in language we are actually visualising our thoughts. This technique involves creating your own unique symbols as a substitute for words. Do not waste time worrying about 'good' drawings – it is more important that the symbols have a unique meaning

to you. The following are important steps to follow when practising this technique:

1. **Write down your problem (challenge) and split it into attributes (parts).**
2. **Write each of these attributes on a separate card. On the other side of the card, draw a symbol (picture) that represents this attribute. The symbols can be simple or intricate – the choice is yours. The use of colours may help you visualise or organise your thoughts more clearly.**
3. **Place all the cards on a table with the symbols facing up. Now start moving them around as you notice relationships, or group some together and see which ideas flow from this unique grouping. Do this for a while.**
4. **Sharpen your wits – start looking for ideas related to your problem. Put cards together which do not seem related in any way to force fresh ideas. Write down some of the ideas which flow from the new combinations.**
5. **If you feel you have not solved the problem to your satisfaction you can, of course, start a new set of cards, listing other attributes of your problem and start the thinking process all over again.**

The effects of thinking development

It has always been accepted that thinking can develop spontaneously because of environmental factors, mentor relationships and countless other stimuli. It is also true that the use of creative techniques can ignite exceptional performance. By becoming familiar with the whole brain techniques discussed in this chapter (and you will find a number of excellent books focusing on creative techniques only) you will be able to deliberately cultivate creativity, and move beyond what you believed to be limitations. Naturally you might find that some of the techniques are more to your liking than others. This is fine, but it is recommended that you develop an understanding of those techniques which are not necessarily in alignment with your thinking preference. This is what whole brain understanding is all about! Sometimes you might feel stupid when trying to apply some of the techniques, while you find others easy. Keep on seeing yourself in a wider perspective and stop feeling insecure.

> Your challenge is not to keep trying to repair what was damaged; your practice instead is to reawaken what is already wise, strong and whole within you; to cultivate those qualities of heart and spirit that are available to you this very moment.
> **– W.Muller –**